IAN C. SCOTT.

IMS (DL/I) DATA-BASE ORGANIZATION AND PERFORMANCE

George U. Hubbard
International Business Machines Corporation
and
Texas Woman's University

IMS (DL/I) DATA-BASE ORGANIZATION AND PERFORMANCE

George U. Hubbard
International Business Machines Corporation
and
Texas Woman's University

VNR VAN NOSTRAND REINHOLD COMPANY ——————————————— New York

Library of Congress Catalog Card Number: 85-20219
ISBN 0-442-23583-6

Manufactured in the United States of America

Published by Van Nostrand Reinhold Company Inc.
115 Fifth Avenue
New York, New York   10003

Van Nostrand Reinhold Company Limited
Molly Millars Lane
Wokingham, Berkshire RG11 2PY, England

Van Nostrand Reinhold
480 Latrobe Street
Melbourne, Victoria 3000, Australia

Macmillan of Canada
Division of Gage Publishing Limited
164 Commander Boulevard
Agincourt, Ontario MIS 3C7, Canada

15   14   13   12   11   10   9   8   7   6   5   4   3   2   1

Library of Congress Cataloging-in-Publication Data

Hubbard, George U.
  IMS (DL/I) data base organization and performance.

  Bibliography: p.
  Includes index.
  1. Data base management.   2. IMS (DL/I) (Computer
system)   I. Title.
QA76.9.D3H84   1986   005.75   85-20219
ISBN 0-442-23583-6

PREFACE

PURPOSE OF THIS BOOK

This book provides, in a readable manner, a detailed understanding of DL/I data bases and how they perform. It is written to help fill a long-standing void in the data-base literature. For persons just entering the data-base arena, there is a wealth of good material to explain the basic concepts. And for the professional practitioner who analyzes data-base performance down to the IWAIT level, excellent tuning guides are available. But there is very little in between. For the person who wants to acquire a good working knowledge of DL/I data bases with emphasis on the performance implications of the various design and tuning choices, very little written help is available.

In one sense, this book might be called a tutorial, but it is more than that. It bridges the gap between a beginning knowledge of DL/I data-base concepts and the very detailed knowledge required for data-base design and tuning studies, and it does this by explaining the major concepts and considerations in data-base organization and performance. It also explains the reasons behind these concepts and considerations so that the reader can then make knowledgeable and reasonable choices and trade-offs in selecting logical and physical design parameters for data-base implementation and tuning. The name of the game is to reduce the number of physical I/Os required to process a job. Minimizing the physical I/Os is accomplished by appropriate data-base and application program design.

After studying this book, the reader should have a good working knowledge of DL/I data-base concepts. The application programmer should be able to devise more efficient DL/I call patterns. The designer and the data-base administrator should be able to make more knowledgeable choices among the numerous options affecting data-base performance. The manager should be better able to give direction and guidance for assuring the quality of the data-base design and performance. And the interested student should gain an increased appreciation and understanding of the complex issues in the world of data bases. Finally, the data-base professional should gain an improved foundation for reading and understanding the detailed data-base performance and tuning guides that are available.

The views expressed in this book are those of the author and do not necessarily represent the views of IBM Corporation. The author assumes full and sole responsibility for its contents. Sincere thanks go to John Dees of IBM and to Dr. Stuart Varden of Pace University for their time spent in reviewing this book and for their many helpful suggestions.

INTENDED AUDIENCE

This book is addressed to practitioners in the areas of data-base design, performance, and tuning. This includes application programmers, data-base designers, data-base administrators, system programmers, and systems analysts. It also includes technical managers who want a clear understanding of the concepts and issues involved. This book can also serve as a textbook for upper division or graduate level college courses dealing with data-base organization, design, and performance.

The material presented here will be more easily understood by readers who already have an elementary familiarity with the structures of DL/I data bases and with the DL/I calls of application programs; this is, however, not an absolute requirement. Those who are already familiar with DL/I may choose to skip Part I and begin directly with Part II.

GEORGE U. HUBBARD

CONTENTS

PART I
INTRODUCTION TO
DL/I DATA BASES

1
OVERVIEW OF DL/I DATA BASES

THE HIERARCHICAL MODEL

Suppose we want to keep and process information about employees, their skills, and their education and experience pertaining to each of their skills. We want each data-base record to contain all of this information for a given employee—that is, there is to be one data-base record per employee. Because each data-base record contains four different categories of information, we will divide the record into four types of informational segments. Each segment will contain the fields that pertain to a particular type of information within the record. For the example at hand, there will be a NAME segment describing the employee, some SKILL segments describing the employee's skills, and some EXPERIENCE and EDUCATION segments describing those respective aspects of each of the employee's skills. An example of a data-base record segmented in this manner is shown in Figure 1-1.

Figure 1-2 shows the same segment organization of the data-base record, but in a more generalized manner. Instead of showing all of the fields within each segment, it shows the overall segments and merely indicates the type of information contained in each segment. The segment type is specified and the key field value is also shown. Note also that each segment is numbered starting with the first segment, which is the root segment. These numbers give the hierarchical sequence of the segments.

Another way of depicting the segment structure of the data-base record is shown in Figure 1-3. This method of presentation shows more clearly the hierarchical, tree-like structure by which the segments of the data-base record are related. The hierarchical sequence numbers are shown in the upper left-hand corners of the segments.

NAME	ADDRESS	CITY	
ADAMS	110 OAK ST.	IRVING	NAME Segment

SKILL	RATING	YEARS	
ARTIST	A	5	SKILL Segment

COURSE	SCHOOL	GRADE	
ART	STANFORD	A	EDUC Segment
DRAFTING	HARVARD	B	EDUC Segment
PORTRAITS	UCLA	A	EDUC Segment

PROJECT	DATES	MANAGER	
SANDIA	1980–81	MURPHY	EXPR Segment
REDSTONE	1976–80	SMITH	EXPR Segment

SKILL	RATING	YEARS	
WRITER	B	2	SKILL Segment

COURSE	SCHOOL	GRADE	
COMPOSITION	HOFSTRA	C	EDUC Segment

PROJECT	DATES	MANAGER	
ARGUS	1975–76	BOONE	EXPR Segment
SATURN	1975	TURNER	EXPR Segment
MERCURY	1974–75	COLE	EXPR Segment

Figure 1–1. A data-base record divided into segments.

Notice that the pattern of the hierarchical sequence is from top to bottom, left to right, and front to back.

One of the fundamental purposes of the segment structure is to provide an efficient means of storing records that contain varying numbers of segments, and also to provide a convenient means of adding or deleting segments. As an example, if Adams acquires new skills, we would like to add additional·SKILL segments (in hierarchical sequence) to his data-base record. If he works on additional projects, we would like to add additional EXPERIENCE segments under the appropriate skills. We need a stable way of depicting the overall segment structure while allowing the number of occurrences of the various segment types to change. In addition, the data-base

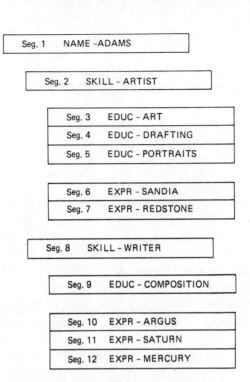

```
Seg. 1    NAME –ADAMS

  Seg. 2    SKILL – ARTIST

      Seg. 3    EDUC – ART
      Seg. 4    EDUC – DRAFTING
      Seg. 5    EDUC – PORTRAITS

      Seg. 6    EXPR – SANDIA
      Seg. 7    EXPR – REDSTONE

  Seg. 8    SKILL – WRITER

      Seg. 9    EDUC – COMPOSITION

      Seg. 10   EXPR – ARGUS
      Seg. 11   EXPR – SATURN
      Seg. 12   EXPR – MERCURY
```

Figure 1–2. Generalized segment structure.

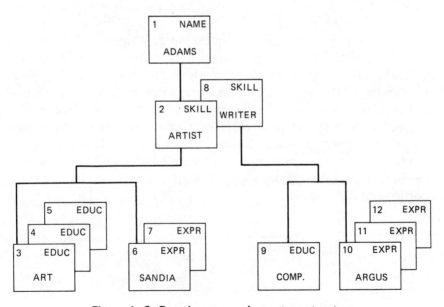

Figure 1–3. Data-base record as a tree structure.

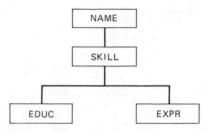

Figure 1–4. Generalized representation of a data-base record.

record for a different employee, while adhering to the same overall segment structure, may have a different number of segment occurrences. For example, Jones may have four or five skills compared with two for Adams. The stable, generalized way of depicting the segment structure of the employee data-base records is shown in Figure 1–4. The interpretation of this representation is that for a given NAME segment (root) there can be any number (including 0) of SKILL segments; and for each SKILL segment there can be any number of EDUCATION segments and also any number of EXPERIENCE segments. In addition, every non-root segment occurrence is the child of a unique parent segment.

DL/I maintains hierarchical sequencing of segments in two ways, depending on the storage organization used. In the sequential storage organizations, hierarchical sequence is maintained by the physical positioning of the segments on the storage device. In the direct storage organizations, the segments can be physically stored in randomly selected locations, and hierarchical sequence is maintained by pointers in the segment prefixes. These pointers enable DL/I to locate a segment of interest according to its hierarchical relationship regardless of its physical location. Figure 1–5 illustrates the prefix and data portions of a segment.

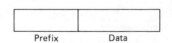

Prefix   Data

Figure 1–5. Segment organization of prefix and data.

ACCESS METHODS

General

A basic understanding of the characteristics of the major DL/I access methods is crucial to an understanding of DL/I data-base performance issues. Choosing the right access method for a given processing environment is one of the most important of all the physical design choices.

There are two basic storage organizations for DL/I data bases, and two major variations of each organization. This results in four basic DL/I access methods. These DL/I access methods, along with the operating system access methods used for implementing them, are represented in Figure 1-6. Although DL/I has some additional special-purpose access methods, we will discuss only the four basic

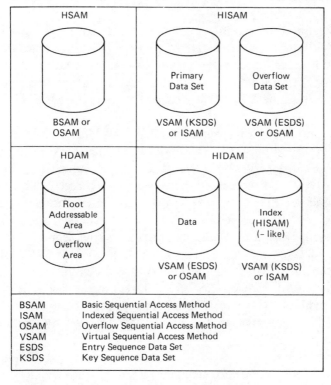

Figure 1–6. Overview of major DL/I access methods.

ones. The two storage organizations are Hierarchical Sequential (HS) and Hierarchical Direct (HD).

In the *Hierarchical Sequential* (*HS*) storage organization, segments within a data-base record are accessed sequentially according to their hierarchical sequence. The Hierarchical Sequential Access Method (HSAM) and the Hierarchical Indexed Sequential Access Method (HISAM) are the two access methods for this organization.

There are two major differences between HSAM and HISAM. First, these two access methods have significantly different ways of beginning their search for a desired segment. HISAM is oriented to searching for segments within a given data-base record (i.e., segments under a given root). It begins its search by referencing an index based on the key (sequence field) value of the root segment of a desired data-base record, to find the physical location of that root. Accessing begins at that root and proceeds sequentially segment-by-segment in hierarchical sequence, for all dependent segments of that root.

HSAM, on the other hand, is not oriented to reading within a particular data-base record. HSAM's orientation is the entire data base, and it begins a series of accesses by starting with the first root segment of the entire data base and proceeding segment-by-segment through the data base just as if a sequential tape file were being processed.

The second major difference between HSAM and HISAM is that HISAM permits updates to the data base while HSAM does not.

In the *Hierarchical Direct* (*HD*) storage organization, segments within a data base record are accessed more directly. The Hierarchical Direct Access Method (HDAM) and the Hierarchical Indexed Direct Access Method (HIDAM) are the two access methods for this organization. Both are oriented toward accessing segments within a particular data-base record, as is HISAM. But HDAM and HIDAM differ from HISAM in that after locating the root segment of the desired data-base record, they use pointers in the segment prefixes (pointers will be described in Chapter 11) to proceed more directly to a desired segment than the sequential, segment-by-segment approach.

A major difference between HDAM and HIDAM lies in their methods of finding the root segment. HIDAM finds the desired root segment by referencing an index based on key values of the roots.

HDAM finds the root segment by a randomizing process of manipulating the key value and transforming it into a physical address by which the root segment can be located. This randomizing process is sometimes called *hashing*. Other major differences involve the physical location of segments on the storage device, but the accessing of segments via pointers is the same after locating the root.

Accessing Overview

At the overview level, we will use a specific example to illustrate the major differences in the four basic DL/I access methods by noting the ways in which they locate a desired segment. Other differences in storage patterns and performance characteristics will be explored later in the detailed treatment of each access method. Consider the three data-base records depicted as hierarchies in Figure 1–7.

These segments, arranged horizontally in hierarchical sequence, yield the pattern partially shown in Figure 1–8. An explanation of the segment naming convention may be helpful. D223, for example, is the third occurrence of a Type D segment under C22, and C22 is the second occurrence of the Type C segment under A2.

Now suppose that segment D223 is to be accessed. Note that D223 is a child of C22, which in turn is a child of root A2, and assume that these relationships are made known to the DL/I search proce-

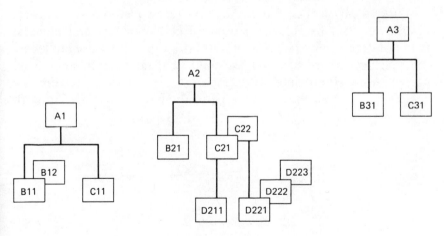

Figure 1–7. Three data-base records.

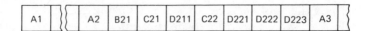

Figure 1-8. Hierarchical storage pattern of segments.

dures. The following sections explain how HSAM, HISAM, HDAM, and HIDAM locate segment D223.

HSAM and HISAM. HSAM always begins its search at the beginning of the data base. In this case, HSAM begins with root A1 and then scans each subsequent segment until C22 under A2, and D223 under C22, are encountered. Accessing segments in data-base records toward the end of the data base can become very costly when the search must begin with the first segment in the data base.

HISAM, on the other hand, begins by searching its index to find the physical location of segment A2, D223's root, and it then makes access directly to A2. HISAM then examines each segment subsequent to A2 in hierarchical order to locate C22 and then D223 under C22.

Figure 1-9 illustrates the accessing patterns of HSAM and HISAM.

HDAM and HIDAM. Before explaining how the HD access methods work, it is necessary to introduce two of the pointer types that may be contained in HD segment prefixes. A full treatment of pointers will be given in Chapter 11.

Within a physical data base, the HD access methods search for a desired segment by following physical child pointers and physical twin pointers. A physical child pointer (Figure 1-10) is used to locate the first occurrence of a desired child segment type under a given parent. A physical twin pointer (Figure 1-11) is used to go from one occurrence of a given segment type to the next occurrence. In both

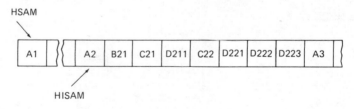

Figure 1-9. HSAM and HISAM accessing.

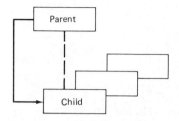

Figure 1–10. Physical child pointer.

the HD access methods, DL/I locates a desired segment by working its way from the root (or from its current position within the record) to the desired segment by following the appropriate physical child pointer when it needs to go down a level, and by following physical twin pointers from left to right to locate the correct segment occurrence within each level.

Figure 1–12 illustrates the accessing patterns of HDAM and HIDAM. After locating the appropriate root, A2, both access methods will proceed to D223 in essentially the same manner. Using the appropriate physical child pointer in the prefix of the root segment, DL/I locates the first occurrence of the next segment type encountered in the path from the root to the desired segment. In this example, DL/I goes directly from the root, A2, to C21. Because D223 is not a dependent of C21, DL/I now follows physical twin pointers in the prefixes of the type C segments until it finds the type C occurrence that defines the path leading downward to the desired segment. In this Case, DL/I goes from C21 to C22. The desired segment, D223, is a child of C22. From C22, DL/I now follows another physical child pointer to the first occurrence of its dependent type D segments, D221 in this case. Then by means of physical twin pointers

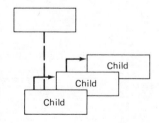

Figure 1–11. Physical twin pointers.

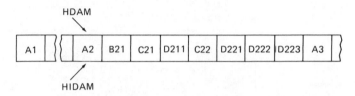

Figure 1–12. HDAM and HIDAM accessing.

in the type D segment prefixes, DL/I follows the type D twin chain from D221 to D222, and then from D222 to D223.

LOGICAL RELATIONS

Logical relations are a means of providing the application programmer with a modified view of a hierarchical structure that can (1) combine segments from more than one physical data base, and/or (2) modify the natural hierarchical structure within a single physical data base. Without logical relations, redundant data or a large amount of searching and sorting could be required to access the segments required by complex applications.

Figure 1-13 shows generalized data-base records from two physical data bases, a NAME data base and a SKILL data base. In the SKILL data base, an application can determine the names of the employees having a particular skill. In the NAME data base, an application can determine the skills possessed by a given employee. The problem is that the SKILL segment is contained in both data bases, and that violates the notion of non-redundancy. Integrity problems, excessive use of storage space, and performance inefficiencies can arise from redundant data. Logical relations can provide a solution.

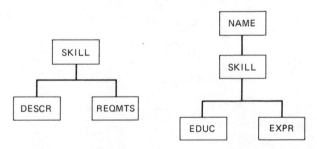

Figure 1–13. Generalized data-base records from two physical data bases.

Suppose, as shown in Figure 1-14, that we remove the data from the SKILL segment in the NAME data base and add another pointer to the prefix of that segment to point to a SKILL segment in the SKILL data base. We can do this if that SKILL segment contains the same fields and values that would have been in the SKILL segment of the NAME data base. Then DL/I's support of logical relations will still enable a program to start with NAME in the NAME data base and find all the skills recorded for that employee. As DL/I accesses what would have been the SKILL segment under NAME, it recognizes that it is now a pointer segment, and it follows the appropriate pointer to the corresponding SKILL segment in the SKILL data base, where it obtains the desired Skill information. DL/I then provides this information to the application program just as if the information had been in the pointer (former SKILL) segment. The pointer segment is a physical child of the NAME segment in the NAME data base, and it is called a logical child of the SKILL segment in the SKILL data base. The SKILL segment in the SKILL data base is called a logical parent of the pointer segment.

Thus far, we have described a logical relation as providing the ability to travel in one direction. In our example (Figure 1-14), we travel from NAME to SKILL. This provides the ability for an application to find all the skills possessed by an employee even though the NAME and SKILL segments are in different physical data bases. This is an example of a *unidirectional* logical relation. Additional pointers are necessary to provide an access path in the opposite direction—that is, from SKILL to NAME. A logical relation that provides the ability to travel in both directions is called a *bidirectional* logical relation. There are two types of a bidirectional logical relations, characterized

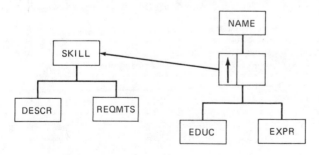

Figure 1-14. Example of a logical relation.

by the terms *virtual pairing* and *physical pairing*. All three types of logical relations are depicted in Figure 1–15.

The two types of bidirectional logical relations exist primarily for performance reasons. With virtual pairing, there is only one logical child segment to update; whereas with physical pairing, if one logical child segment is updated, a corresponding logical child in the other data base must similarly be updated to preserve synchronization. For reasons that will be explored in Chapters 9 and 11, physical pairing can be expected to provide faster accessing for retrievals. With regard to space, virtual pairing requires less storage space than physical pairing, because there are only half as many logical child segments.

Using logical relations to combine physical data bases enables the application programmer to treat the combination as though it were a single hierarchy called a logical data base. Using the example of Figure 1–14 and considering the logical relation to be bidirectional, the application programmer can work with a logical data base starting with the root segment NAME, as shown in Figure 1–16, or with a different logical data base starting with the root segment SKILL, as shown in Figure 1–17.

SECONDARY INDEXING

Secondary indexing makes it possible to access segment occurrances of a data base in some order other than their sequence field values, and to enter a data base through some segment other than the root segment. A secondary index is actually a separate HISAM-like data base containing segments consisting of the values of the key field to be used and pointers to the segments to be accessed. The segment to be accessed is called the *target* segment. The segment con-

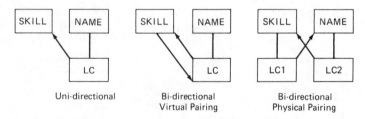

Figure 1–15. Types of logical relations.

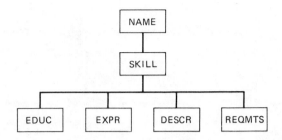

Figure 1-16. Logical data base starting with **NAME**.

taining the key field to be used is called the *source* segment. The segments of the secondary index are called *pointer* segments. The key field to be used may be another field (other than the sequence field) in the target segment, or it may be any field in a lower-level segment.

Figure 1-18 shows three examples of secondary indexes. In Figure 1-18a, the root segment is both the target and the source segment. Suppose the sequence field of the NAME segment is EMP-NO, but we want to access the NAME segments in some order other than employee number, say by zip code. Assuming ZIP-CODE is also a field in the NAME segments, a secondary index can contain pointer segments of ZIP-CODE values and pointers to all the target NAME segments containing those zip-code values. Such a secondary index enables an application program to access the NAME segments in zip-code order (or for a particular group of zip-codes) rather than in employee number order.

Similarly, any field in a dependent segment may be used as a source

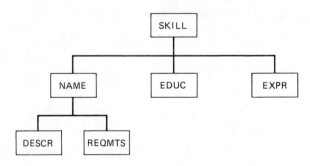

Figure 1-17. Logical data base starting with **SKILL**.

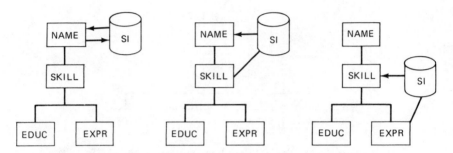

Figure 1-18. Examples of secondary indexing.

key. Figure 1-18b illustrates a secondary index for accessing the NAME segments in order by skills. Thus, for each skill, the secondary index contains pointer segments pointing to the NAME segments for all employees possessing that skill.

Figure 1-18c shows that the target segment need not be the root segment—that is, the entry to the data base may be made at any segment. But when this is done, the target segment appears to the application program as a root segment in a restructured (logical) view of the data base. Again, the application program deals with a logical data base rather than a physical data base. Figure 1-19 shows the logical data base that would result from the secondary index example of Figure 1-18c.

DBDs AND PSBs

Means must be provided for the application programs to communicate with the data base without being aware of the physical location of the segments on the storage devices. In addition, because of the integrated data-base concept, means must be provided to restrict

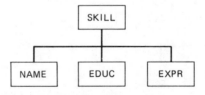

Figure 1-19. Logical data base from secondary indexing.

application programs from access to unauthorized segments or fields. Data Base Descriptors (DBDs) and Program Specification Blocks (PSBs) are the means of accomplishing these objectives. A DBD describes the content and hierarchical structure of an entire physical or logical data base, and it provides the information DL/I needs to locate the desired segments. Additionally, the choice of access method is specified in the DBD.

A PSB specifies which of the data base segments a particular application program is authorized to access. Because an application program may access more than one data base, the PSB is composed of one or more Program Control Blocks (PCBs). Each PCB defines a program's authorization to segments within a particular data base. A further function of the PCB is to contain certain types of feedback information so that the program and also the DL/I system can determine the results of each DL/I call. The relationships of DBDs, PSBs, PCBs, data bases, and application programs is shown in Figure 1–20.

Figure 1–20a shows three PCBs associated, through three DBDs, with three data bases. Each PCB contains the name of the DBD through which its data-base association is established. Each PCB keeps its own record of parentage, positioning, and other accessing information pertaining to the processing of its associated data base.

Frequently it is desirable to process the same data base from more than one perspective. For example, a program may want to do concurrent processing in two or more portions of the data base in such

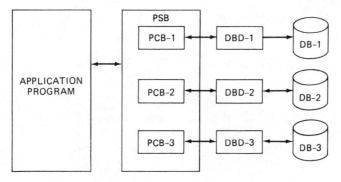

Figure 1–20a. Normal relationship of DBDs, PSBs, PCBs, data bases, and application programs.

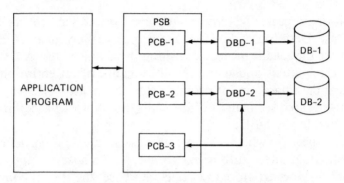

Figure 1–20b. Relationship of DBDs, PCBs, PCBs, data bases, and application programs illustrating the use of two PCBs for the same data base.

a way that positioning, parentage, and so on, are retained and used for each of these portions. This may be accomplished by naming the same DBD in two or more PCBs, as is illustrated in Figure 1–20b. By this means, the application program has two (or more) independent windows into the same data base.

PART II
PERFORMANCE ASPECTS OF
DL/I ACCESS METHODS

2
HIERARCHICAL SEQUENTIAL ACCESS METHOD—HSAM

DESCRIPTION

A HSAM data base is a series of blocked segments loaded in hierarchical sequence. Updates are not permitted; therefore, this sequence does not change. Updates can be made, as with tape files, by copying the data base.

HSAM blocks are fixed length with no distinction between primary and overflow blocks. The four data base records of Figure 2-1 would be loaded into successive blocks as shown in Figure 2-2.

HSAM PERFORMANCE CHARACTERISTICS

HSAM is very fast for reading a data base sequentially, but because it has no update capability, it is rarely used in normal application program processing. It is a good access method for reading a sequential file or for creating a sequential file. HSAM is a good candidate for reading or writing historical-type data. It also should be considered for sequential processing of a stable, root-only data base.

In addition to not being able to update, HSAM also cannot begin its search at a specified root segment; it must begin at the beginning of the data base. Thus HSAM is truly a sequential access method with no direct access or indexed access capability. It supports tape as well as disk I/O.

Summary of HSAM Characteristics

HSAM has advantages as well as disadvantages. Its major advantages are as follows:

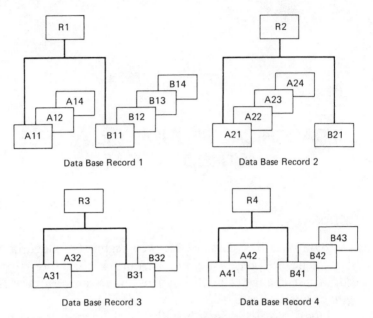

Figure 2–1. **Data-base record examples.**

1. HSAM is the only DL/I access method supporting tape devices.
2. Conversion from OS data sets is relatively easy.
3. HSAM is relatively fast for purely sequential reads (existing data base) or inserts (new data base).

The major disadvantages of HSAM are as follows:

1. In order to update a data base it must be rewritten.
2. Logical relations and secondary indexing are not available.
3. No access directly to a given root segment is possible.

R1	A11	A12	A14	B11	B12	B13

B14	R2	A21	A22	A23	A24	B21

R3	A31	A32	B31	B32	R4	A41

A42	B41	B42	B43			

Figure 2–2. **Loading of data-base records R1, R2, R3, and R4 using HSAM.**

3
HIERARCHICAL INDEXED SEQUENTIAL ACCESS METHOD—HISAM

DESCRIPTION

A HISAM data base is composed of two separate, physical data sets: a *primary* data set, and an *overflow* data set (Figure 3-1). Each data set is noted in the Job Control Language (JCL) by a Data Definition (DD) statement. Physical parent–child relationships and hierarchical sequence of segments are maintained normally by the physical adjacency of the segments. However, we shall see that when segments must be placed into the overflow data set, chains between the primary and overflow data sets are also needed to maintain relationships and sequencing.

Primary Data Set

The primary data set is implemented as a Keyed Sequence Data Set (KSDS) using the Virtual Storage Access Method (VSAM) or by the Indexed Sequential Access Method (ISAM). The primary data set

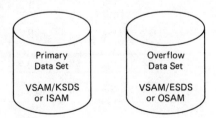

Primary
Data Set

VSAM/KSDS
or ISAM

Overflow
Data Set

VSAM/ESDS
or OSAM

Figure 3-1. General organization of a HISAM data base.

contains both the index and many of the data segments. The storage space for data is divided into blocks (or VSAM Control Intervals—CIs) which are in turn subdivided into logical records (Figure 3-2). The block is the unit of information transferred between main storage the I/O device when a physical I/O occurs.

In the primary data set, one and only one logical record is used for storing a data-base record. The logical record receives a root segment and as many dependent segments, in hierarchical sequence, as will fit. Additional dependent segments for that data-base record will go into one or more logical records in the overflow data set.

Optimal logical-record size is elusive and very difficult to ascertain. Since the majority of accessing is expected to be in the primary data set, the primary logical record should be large enough to contain the segments most likely to be accessed. Otherwise, physical I/Os to overflow blocks and then back again to the primary blocks may be required for accessing additional segments.

With regard to space considerations, logical records can be too big, and they can also be too little. Space can be wasted in both situations. In the primary data set, there is never a need for the logical record to be larger than the full data-base record. But since data-base records typically contain varying numbers of segments, logical records large enough for the largest data-base records are wasteful of space for all shorter data base records. On the other hand, logical records that are too short contain a different kind of waste space. Here we have the increased likelihood of waste space because the remaining space is not large enough for the next segment. In such cases, the remaining segments go into the overflow data set.

As a rule of thumb, the length of the primary logical record is

LR 1	LR 2	LR 3	LR 4	LR 5

LR 1	LR 2	LR 3	LR 4	LR 5

LR 1	LR 2	LR 3	LR 4	LR 5

LR 1	LR 2	LR 3	LR 4	LR 5

Figure 3-2. Four blocks (or control intervals) containing five logical records each.

usually chosen to accommodate (1) the average-sized data-base record or (2) the most frequently used portion of the record.

Overflow Data Set

The overflow data set is implemented as an Entry Sequence Data Set (ESDS) of VSAM, or as an Overflow Sequential Data Set (OSAM). A VSAM/ESDS overflow data set is usually used with a VSAM/KSDS primary data set, although it is possible (and sometimes advantageous) to use a VSAM/KSDS–OSAM combination.

As has been stated, dependent segments that will not fit into a primary logical record are placed into logical records of the overflow data set. This is true of initial load and also when inserting after initial load. In addition, if the primary data set uses the ISAM access method, all segments, including root segments, that are inserted after initial load are placed into the overflow data set, where they will remain until a reorganization occurs. The ISAM root segment and as many of its dependents as will fit will go into the first available logical record in the overflow data set. The remaining dependent segments will go into succeeding logical records.

The overflow logical record must be at least as large as the primary logical record, and its size selection involves a trade-off between processing efficiency and storage space. The larger the overflow logical record, the less likely that additional blocks will have to be accessed to obtain the desired segments of a given data-base record.

With regard to space considerations, an optimal logical record size is elusive and very difficult to ascertain. Logical records that are longer or shorter than the optimal are wasteful of space but for different reasons. Long logical records will waste space if there are not enough segments in the data-base records to fill them. Short logical records can waste space because as they become nearly filled, the remaining space is frequently not large enough for the next segment. Short logical records mean more logical records, which in turn means more of this type of waste space.

HISAM STORAGE PATTERNS

The following sections demonstrate how segments are stored into a HISAM data base. To illustrate these examples, the data-base records depicted in Figure 3–3 will be used.

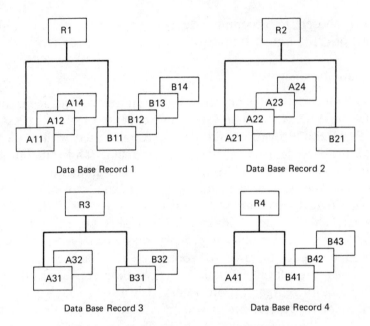

Figure 3–3. Data-base record Examples.

Initial Loading

Regardless of whether VSAM/KSDS or ISAM is used, initial loading follows the same general pattern. A root segment and as many dependent segments as will fit are loaded into a primary data set logical record. Any remaining dependent segments are loaded into the first available overflow logical record and into subsequent overflow logical records as needed. Relationships and sequencing between the primary segments and the overflow segments are maintained by pointers within the logical records. Figure 3–4 illustrates the initial loading of data-base records R1 and R4 from the structures depicted in Figure 3–3. For simplicity in these examples, we will assume three logical records per block in the primary data set, and four logical records per block in the overflow data set. We will assume that all segment types are the same size, that four segments will fit into a primary logical record, and that three segments will fit into an overflow logical record.

Primary Data Set
(Three Logical Records per CI)

R1	A11	A12	A14
R4	A41	A42	B41

Overflow Data Set
(Four Logical Records per CI)

B11	B12	B13
B14		
B42	B43	

Figure 3–4. Initial loading of data-base records R1 and R4.

Inserting Root Segments After Initial Load

The pattern for inserting root segments after initial load differs depending on whether VSAM/KSDS or ISAM is used in the primary data set. When discussing the VSAM implementation of HISAM, we shall refer to blocks as *Control Intervals* (*CIs*). When discussing the ISAM/OSAM implementation, we shall use the term *blocks*.

Using VSAM/KSDS, HISAM inserts the new root into an appropriate primary logical record so that its physical location places it in key sequence with the roots on its immediate left and right. If necessary, segments in logical records to the right of the insertion point are actually moved to the right into new logical records, to free the appropriate logical record for the new root.

Assuming a VSAM/KSDS primary data set with logical records available in the appropriate CI, Figure 3-5 shows the results of inserting data-base record R2 into the data base initially loaded with R1 and R4.

If all the logical records in the appropriate CI are already full, something called a CI-split occurs in the VSAM/KSDS primary data set. A new CI is obtained, and about half (the right half) of the logical records in the filled CI are physically moved into the new CI. Now there is available room in both CIs, and the new root can be inserted in physical sequence.

Figure 3-6 illustrates the results of inserting data-base record R3 into a primary CI that has already been filled with R1, R2, and R4.

For an ISAM primary data set, the insertion of root segments follows a different pattern. For this example, Figure 3-7 illustrates the insertion of data-base record R2 after the data base has been initially

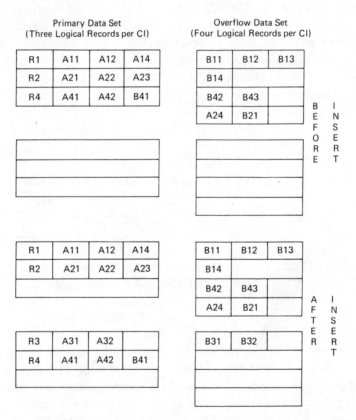

Figure 3–5. Insertion of new data-base record (R2) using VSAM with room available in the CI.

Figure 3–6. Insertion of new data-base record (R3) using VSAM with no room available in the CI.

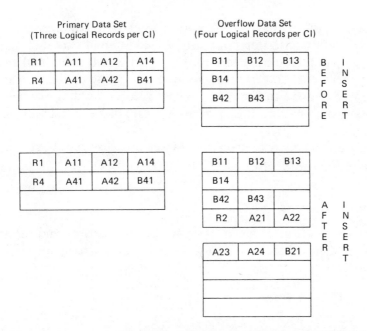

Figure 3-7. Insertion of new data-base record (R2) using ISAM/OSAM.

loaded with R1 and R4. Note that in the ISAM example (Figure 3-7), R2 is in the overflow data set, while in VSAM example (Figure 3-5), R2 was placed into the primary data set.

The concept of CI-splits occurs with VSAM but not ISAM. With ISAM, all inserted roots go into the overflow data set, and key sequence is maintained by pointers. Thus the new root and as many dependent segments as will fit are inserted into the first available logical record in the overflow data set. Additional dependent segments, if any, go into subsequent logical records in the overflow data set.

Inserting Dependent Segments

Dependent segments are inserted in the same way regardless of whether VSAM or ISAM/OSAM is used. Dependent segments are inserted physically in hierarchical sequence. Segments to the right of the insertion point may be moved to the right to make room for the segment being inserted. This type of insertion is performed fairly efficiently. But if the logical record is already filled, all segments to the right of the insertion point are pushed out and placed into a new (next available) logical record in the overflow data set to make room for the segment being inserted. By means of pointers, this new logical record is chained to the other logical records holding segments of the same data-base record so as to maintain hierarchical sequence of the segments.

Figure 3–8 shows the results of inserting a segment, A13, into a primary logical record that is already filled.

Deleting Segments

When segments are deleted, the gaps are not closed, and the space is not made available for future updates until a reorganization oc-

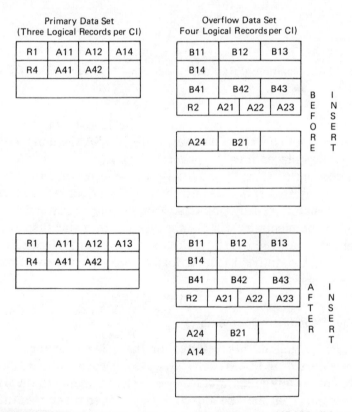

Figure 3–8. Insertion of new data-base record (A13) using VSAM with no room available in the logical record.

curs. The delete byte is simply turned on. The delete bytes in dependents of the deleted segment are not turned on, but these dependents, along with the deleted parent, are not available for further processing. (DL/I still has to search through them when accessing a segment further down in hierarchical order.) There is one exception to the above rule. Using VSAM, if a root segment is deleted, and if neither it nor its dependents are involved in a logical relationship, the contents of that logical record are physically deleted and the space is made available for future use. But any dependents of that root that are in the overflow data set are not erased, and their space is not made available until the data base is reorganized.

Replacing Segments

The replacement of fixed-length segments occurs in a very straightforward manner following their retrieval. Replacing variable-length segments becomes a problem if the segment has expanded; this will be discussed in the section "Implications of Variable-Length Segments" later in this chapter.

LOGICAL RELATIONS

Logical relations and secondary indexing have limited implementations in HISAM data bases. Uni-directional logical relations and bi-directional logical relations with physical pairing can be implemented in HISAM, but bi-directional logical relations with virtual pairing cannot be implemented because it requires four-byte direct pointers. For the same reason, pointer options such as backward pointers are also unavailable. Finally, logical children in a HD data base that reference logical parents in a HISAM data base must do so with symbolic pointers.

SECONDARY DATA SET GROUPS

In HISAM data bases, secondary data set groups must begin with a second level segment and must also contain all of its dependent segment types. Thus secondary data set groups in HISAM do not have the freedom of containing any segment type as they can in HDAM and HIDAM. On the other hand, an application program may access directly into a HISAM secondary data set group. This can save the time that would otherwise be required to pass through the root segment.

HISAM PERFORMANCE CHARACTERISTICS

HISAM's primary advantage is that it performs very well for sequential processing of a well-organized data base. In fact, under favorable conditions, HISAM can outperform HDAM and HIDAM. This is largely because HISAM accesses do not require the overhead of processing and following prefix pointers. Also, because HISAM does not employ free space, its blocks are likely to be more densely packed. A lesser reason is also that HISAM segments have shorter prefixes than HDAM or HIDAM segments, which means that HISAM segments may be even more tightly packed to a slight extent.

But as inserts occur and segments are placed into the HISAM overflow data set, performance degrades. This is because several blocks may be accessed in the processing of a single data-base record (for an example, see Figure 3-8). Each block accessed means an additional physical I/O if the block is not already in the buffer pool. In addition, unclaimed space from deleted segments serves to force new inserts into additional blocks.

Because of its reliance on physical adjacency, HISAM performs best when the root key values are uniformly distributed. When inserting roots whose key values are clustered, empty space in that portion of the data base tends to become used up and CI splits become more likely, even though ample empty space still exists in other portions of the data base.

Thus for well organized data bases in which the processing is predominately sequential and the root key values are well distributed, HISAM gives relatively good performance. But as inserts and deletes occur, the performance degrades until a reorganization is required to reclaim unused space and to rearrange the segments so that physical adjacent sequence is maximized and chains to and from the overflow area are minimized.

It should be noted that although it is the logical records that are linked together by pointers, accessing requires a new physical I/O only when a link leads to a new block. And if the new block is already in a memory buffer (highly unlikely when doing sequential processing), a physical I/O is also avoided.

Summary of HISAM Characteristics

The major advantages of HISAM are as follows:

1. Sequential retrieval without using the index can be relatively fast if the data base is well organized.
2. Direct access is provided, via an index, to root segments of a sequential file.
3. Faster loading is possible than with HD organizations—somewhat faster than HIDAM because a separate index data base is not involved, and significantly faster than HDAM because random arm movement is avoided.

The major disadvantages of HISAM are as follows:

1. Using ISAM/OSAM, all inserts go into the overflow data set, although with VSAM root segments go into the primary data set.
2. No direct pointers exist to the root or to the other segments.
3. Segments are physically moved to make room for inserts.
4. Deleted segment space is not immediately available for use.
5. Logical relationships are somewhat restricted (e.g., no virtual pairing).
6. Clustered values of root keys tend to degrade performance as new roots are inserted.

IMPLICATIONS OF VARIABLE-LENGTH SEGMENTS

In HISAM if a segment being replaced is larger than its original size, one or more segments to its right will be relocated to the overflow data set to make the necessary room available. Thus additional chains to and from the overflow data set are created, and accessing these displaced segments will be slower.

If a segment decreases in size, segments will be moved within its logical record to maintain physical adjacency.

SUMMARY OF HISAM DESIGN PARAMETERS

In this section we will review the design parameters directly associated with HISAM and discuss the performance implications of each of them. Even here, the number of interrelationships and trade-offs causes us to give general considerations rather than concrete choices.

The parameters discussed are logical record size and CI (block) size. These are coded directly into the DBD, and are specified separately for the primary and the overflow data sets.

Logical Record Size

Primary Logical Record. The primary logical record size (LRECL) is probably the most important of the HISAM design parameters.

The sequential processing of segments in the primary logical record proceeds very rapidly; therefore the primary logical record should be long enough to hold a root and those dependent segments that will be most frequently accessed. And it must be at least as long as the longest segment. If a distinction can be made between frequently and infrequently accessed segments, consider choosing a logical record size in the primary data set so as to force the infrequently accessed segments into the overflow data set. This serves the dual purpose of keeping the frequently used segments together in the primary logical records and also of having as many data-base records as possible represented within a given primary block. Of course, this arrangement begins to break down as inserts occur.

Instead of choosing the logical record size for the frequently accessed segments, it could be chosen large enough to hold the entire data-base record. This would provide the best performance because physical I/Os to and from the overflow data set would be avoided. If the data-base records are approximately the same size, this is a good option to consider. But if they are of significantly varying sizes, this option could be quite wasteful of storage space, because every data-base record except the longest would fit into a logical record with waste space to spare. A popular rule of thumb is to try to choose logical record sizes so as to hold about 70 percent of the most active segments.

Overflow Logical Record. As has been explained, the overflow logical record size involves a trade-off between performance and space. The choice is not so critical as that of the primary logical record.

CI (Block) Size

For VSAM implementations of HISAM, longer blocks in the primary data set can mean more logical records per block and a smaller number of blocks. This usually means a performance advantage because more roots can be accessed with a single physical I/O. But longer blocks can have a slight negative impact on insertion activity, because when logical records must be moved to make room for an insertion, it is possible that more logical records will have to be moved. In addition, because longer blocks can mean a smaller number of blocks, it is possible that there are fewer empty blocks available to receive CI-splits. With HISAM, block lengths are usually as long as possible consistent with track and buffer pool sizes.

4
HIERARCHICAL DIRECT ACCESS METHOD— HDAM

DESCRIPTION

The physical storage of an HDAM data base is organized into two areas: a *Root Addressable Area* (*RAA*) and an *Overflow area*. These two areas are logical subdivisions of a single data set, and therefore have the same block size and free space characteristics. An HDAM data base is implemented as a single VSAM ESDS or an OSAM data set.

The general organization of the HDAM storage organization is depicted in Figure 4-1. Until we talk about data set groups (in Chapter 8), we will think of an HDAM data base as a single data set in which all blocks (RAA and Overflow) are the same size. Refer to Figure 1-6 for the general organization of an HDAM data base in relation to the other three major DL/I access methods.

Root Addressable Area (RAA)

In the Root Addressable Area, the portion of each block that is available for storing segments is divided into logical units that we shall call *slots*. These slots are of variable length but of a maximum size as specified by the byte limit parameter in the HDAM DBD, and their existence is determined dynamically as root segments are loaded or inserted. Each slot is defined as the space required for storing one root segment and as many of its dependent segments (in hierarchical order) as will fit into the number of bytes specified by the byte limit parameter. The next root to go into a block will be placed immediately following the previous slot. The slots, therefore, are not necessarily all of the same length, because short records may not fill the

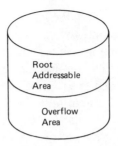

Figure 4-1. General organization of an HDAM data base.

maximum available slot size. Dependent segments that cannot fit into a RAA slot are placed into the Overflow area.

Root Anchor Point (RAP)

Each RAA block also contains a number of *Root Anchor Points* (*RAPs*). A Root Anchor Point is used to locate a particular slot, and it contains the physical location of the slot with which it is associated. When inserting a new root segment, DL/I randomizes the segment's key in such a way that a particular RAA block and a particular RAP within the block are identified. The root segment is placed into an available slot (assuming there is one) in that block, and the location of that slot is placed into the chosen RAP. (We will treat randomizing in more detail later in this chapter.) For locating an existing root segment, the RAP points DL/I to the slot that is expected to contain the desired root.

Figure 4-2 presents a simplified view of HDAM RAA blocks. A

RAP1	RAP2	RAP3	Slot 1	Slot 2	Slot 3	
RAP1	RAP2	RAP3	Slot 1	Slot 2	Slot 3	▨
RAP1	RAP2	RAP3	Slot 1	Slot 2	Slot 3	
RAP1	RAP2	RAP3	Slot 1	Slot 2	Slot 3	
RAP1	RAP2	RAP3	Slot 1	Slot 2	Slot 3	▨
RAP1	RAP2	RAP3	Slot 1	Slot 2	Slot 3	▨

Figure 4-2. HDAM Root Addressable Area of six blocks. Each block contains three RAPs and three slots.

representation of the slots and RAPs is shown, but free space and many overhead fields are omitted.

The number of root anchor points is another DBD parameter, and it is not necessarily equal to the number of slots in a block. There is no direct relation between the number of slots and the number of RAPs in a block, although the number of RAPs should be very close to the expected number of slots. Guidelines will be suggested later in this chapter. If the randomizer does not randomize to certain RAPs in a block, there will be fewer slots than RAPs in that block. On the other hand, we shall see that synonyms can lead to more slots than RAPs in a block. Figure 4-2 depicts a series of blocks containing three slots and three RAPs each. Notice that the slots are of variable length, according to small record size, but of maximum length for large records. The shaded areas indicate waste space that is not large enough to contain additional segments.

Overflow Area

The Overflow blocks are the same size as the RAA blocks, but they are not divided into slots and do not have Root Anchor Points. Segments that do not fit into the RAA slots are placed into the first available space in the Overflow area. Segments that are too large to fit at the end of a block will go into the first position in the next block. A typical representation of an HDAM overflow area is shown in Figure 4-3.

HDAM STORAGE PATTERNS

To illustrate the way segments are stored in an HDAM data base, the data-base records of Figure 4-4 will be used.

Figure 4-3. HDAM Overflow area of four blocks.

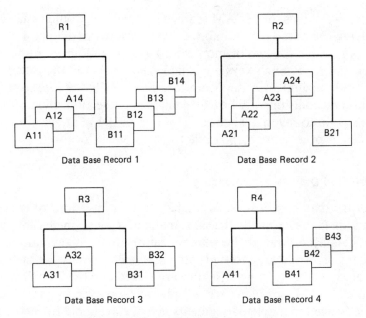

Figure 4-4. Data-base record examples.

Initial Loading

Data-base records are loaded into an HDAM data base in the following manner. The key of the root segment is randomized to a physical location, which is specified in the form of a block number (in the RAA) and a RAP number. The root segment and all the dependent segments that will fit are loaded into the first available slot in the indicated block, and the location of that slot is placed into the indicated RAP. The remaining segments of the record are placed into blocks in the overflow area. Physical child and physical twin pointers are created to establish appropriate connections between segments.

Without explicitly specifying segment sizes, we will assume that the maximum slot size (byte limit) and the segment sizes are such that the following conditions hold:

1. A root and several type A segments will fit into a slot.
2. A root, up to three type A segments, and one type B segment will fit into a slot.
3. Regardless of the number of type A segments, only one type B segment will fit into a slot.

Figure 4–5 shows the HDAM storage pattern that would result from applying the criteria stated above to the records of Figure 4–4.

It is possible for two or more root keys to randomize to the same block and RAP. Such keys are called *synonyms*, and the calculation (by randomizing) of a duplicate location is called a *collision*. Synonyms and collisions will be treated in the next section. It is sufficient at this point to say that when collisions occur, DL/I attempts to place the new root as close as possible to its "home" location.

Inserts and Deletes after Loading

After the data base is initially loaded, further insertions of root segments are made in exactly the same manner. Root segments are placed into slots according to the randomization of their key values. Dependent segments are inserted into the same RAA slot as their root if space is available; otherwise they are placed into the Overflow area. Unlike HISAM, segments are *not* physically moved by insertion activity. Space from deleted segments is made available for new insertions.

Sequential Processing of Roots

While sequential processing of HDAM root segments is possible using a series of GET NEXT calls with unqualified SSAs, the following characteristics should be considered:

1. The roots will be obtained according to their physical locations and not according to key sequence.
2. If ordering by root key sequence is required, it can be obtained

Root Addressable Area (RAA)

RAP1	RAP2	R1	A11	A12	A14	B11	R2	A21	A22	A23	A24

RAP1	RAP2	R3	A31	A32	B31	R4	A41	B41	Available		

Overflow Area

B12	B13	B14	B21	B31	B32	B41	B42	B43	Available		

Figure 4–5. An example of HDAM storage pattern.

by sorting the roots after retrieving them, or by using a randomizer that loads roots so that their physical sequence is also their key sequence.

3. Time is expended while DL/I reads and examines blocks that may be empty.
4. Blocks containing synonyms from other blocks are read and examined twice—once in the normal scan of the blocks, and once when processing the synonym chain.

RANDOMIZING

Synonyms and Collisions

An ideal randomizing (or hashing) algorithm is one that transforms every root segment key into a unique physical storage address so that the roots are uniformly distributed in the allocated storage area with no two roots randomizing to the same location. Ideal randomizing algorithms generally are rare; in actual practice collisions and poor distributions tend to occur. If the randomizer causes a collision by designating a RAP that has already been used, the already filled slot pointed to by the RAP is made to point to another slot that will get the root segment (and its RAA dependents) that we are trying to insert. This is done by means of physical twin pointers in the prefix of the root, with the synonym keys being chained in collating sequence. Thus we have a chaining arrangement for the RAP to its already filled slot and on to the slot that actually receives the root being inserted. This chain is called a *synonym* or *collision chain*. The slot pointed to by a RAP is called a *home address*, and it contains the first root segment that randomized to that block and RAP. The additional slots on the synonym chain, which contain the later roots that randomized to the same block and RAP, are called *synonym addresses*.

Synonym chains are maintained in key sequence. This can mean further performance degradation when inserting into the chains and when searching them.

If the keys of several root segments all randomize to the same block and RAP, the synonym chain can become fairly long, and it may be that several blocks are encountered in following the chain from the RAP to the appropriate slot. Each of these blocks encountered represents an additional physical I/O. Thus long synonym chains can have a significant negative impact on the accessing of HDAM root segments.

A corollary problem of synonyms is that whenever a synonym is placed into some other slot, then another root that should legitimately be placed into that same slot must now go somewhere else. Thus a secondary effect of synonyms is to reduce the number of home locations available for subsequent randomizing.

Randomizer Evaluation

Clustering is a possible effect of randomizing. Some portions of the RAA may become densely filled while other portions remain relatively empty. The objection to clustering is that collisions are more likely to result in the clustered portions of the RAA, while ample space for home locations still exists in the other portions.

Most randomizing algorithms yield good results while the data base is lightly loaded. But as the packing factor increases (i.e., as the data base becomes filled), the effectiveness of the randomizing algorithm tends to deteriorate according to the pattern illustrated in Figure 4-6. In this figure, *packing factor* refers to the ratio of records stored to the maximum record capacity. The vertical axis represents the percentage of randomizations that result in a collision.

For a given distribution of key values, each randomizing technique begins to degrade seriously when a packing factor critical to that technique is reached. Thus the task becomes one of determining

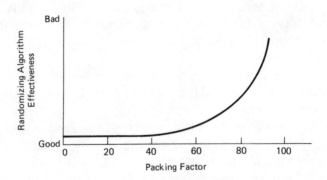

Figure 4-6. Concept of randomizer efficiency.

which of a candidate set of randomizing algorithms will yield the best results at high packing factors.

Computer assistance can be very helpful in evaluating candidate randomizing algorithms. If the expected distributions of the root key values can be ascertained or approximated, then the expected distribution patterns of root segment placement can be calculated and studied for various packing factors and DBD parameters. For example, we would expect that as the packing factor increases, the number of synonym chains will increase and that the lengths of the chains will increase. We would like to compare these growth rates for different randomizing algorithms. The kind of information needed is indicated in Figure 4-7.

Graphic results are also desirable, and these are especially useful with conversational online capabilities. For any of the columns in Figure 4-7, such as the number of synonym chains or average length, the results of various randomizing algorithms can be compared on a single graph (or screen), as shown in Figure 4-8, and variations can be noted as the randomizing parameters are varied.

Finally, a presentation like that shown in Figure 4-9 is effective for visualizing the distribution patterns of the root segments. A visual comparison of the root distribution for each of the randomizing techniques can reveal which technique produces the most favorable storage pattern for the expected key value distributions. Figure 4-9a

| Data Base Name: | Size of RAA: | Byte Limit: |
| Randomizer Name: | No. of RAPs: | Block Size: |

Packing Factor	No. of Synonym chains	Minimum Length	Average Length	Maximum Length	Standard Deviation
10	———	———	———	———	———
20	———	———	———	———	———
30	———	———	———	———	———
40	———	———	———	———	———
50	———	———	———	———	———
60	———	———	———	———	———
70	———	———	———	———	———
80	———	———	———	———	———
90	———	———	———	———	———
100	———	———	———	———	———

Figure 4-7. Display of randomizer characteristics.

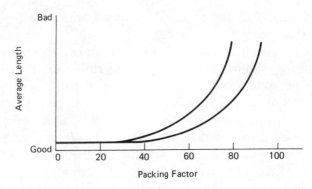

Figure 4–8. Comparative display of randomizer characteristics.

is a binary presentation showing which slots are empty and which
are occupied by randomized root segments. The relative slot addresses are indicated vertically by hundreds and horizontally by units.
In presentations of this type, clustering tendencies are easily de-
tected. Figure 4–9b is a more informative presentation showing, for

						Units						
		0	1	2	3	4	5	6	7	8	9	9
		0	0	0	0	0	0	0	0	0	0	9
	1	1	1		11	11111		11	1	111	11	1
	2		111	1	11111	11		1111		1 1	111	1
Hundreds	3	1 1	11 11	1 1	11		1	1 1	11111	11		11
	4	111111		11 1	111111		111111	1 1 1	1111			
	5		11 1111	1111		1111		111 11		1		

(a)

						Units						
		0	1	2	3	4	5	6	7	8	9	9
		0	0	0	0	0	0	0	0	0	0	9
	1	1	1		11	12111		11	1	311	11	1
	2		111	1	12131	11		1141		1 1	211	2
Hundreds	3	1 3	11 21	1 1	21		1	1 1	12311	11	5	11
	4	132412		11 2	131321		314211	1 3 1	2221			
	5	2 11	3231	1324		11311		2211	13	1		

(b)

Figure 4–9. Displays of home address distribution patterns.

entries greater than one, the length of synonym chains and where they begin.

Watching either of these distribution patterns change as the packing factor increases, which can be done on an interactive display, can be an informative exercise.

HDAM CHARACTERISTICS

One of HDAM's primary advantages is that root segments (excluding the possible synonym problem) can be located quickly with one I/O. Another major advantage is that with at most one additional I/O, DL/I can go from any segment to the first occurrence of a desired dependent segment type at the next level by following the appropriate physical child pointer.

The advantages and disadvantages listed here are derived primarily from *The Data Base Design Guide* published jointly by IBM and the GUIDE International Corporation (Reference 3).

The major advantages of HDAM are as follows:

1. HDAM can have nonunique root segment keys.
2. Space from deleted segments can normally be reused immediately.
3. Segments are not physically moved to make room for inserted segments.
4. A data base may be split into data set groups at any hierarchical level.
5. Random accessing is generally faster than using an index.

The major disadvantages of HDAM are as follows:

1. There is no efficient sequential accessing of root segments. (They can be accessed sequentially, but their keys will be in random order according to their random distribution on the storage device.)
2. Accessing of root segments can be slower than with an index if the randomizing algorithm is not well-suited for the distribution of key values or if root segments are not in their home addresses.
3. HDAM is slower loading than HIDAM or HISAM. Loading

time may be improved by sorting the records into their randomized physical address sequence.

SUMMARY OF HDAM DESIGN PARAMETERS

In this section we will review the design parameters directly associated with HDAM and give the relative advantages and disadvantages relating to them. Even here, the number of interrelationships and trade-offs dictate that general considerations be presented rather than concrete choices.

The following parameters are discussed. All except the size of the Overflow area are directly coded into the DBD.

- Randomizer method
- Number of Root Anchor Points
- Byte limit (size of slots)
- Number of blocks in Root Addressable Area
- Size of Overflow area
- Free space

Randomizer Method

A randomizer technique that yields a uniform distribution of roots with no synonyms is the ideal. If the distribution of root key values can be predicted in advance, candidate randomizing techniques can be evaluated, and the one yielding a distribution closest to being uniform (and with the least number of synonyms) can be selected.

Number of Root Anchor Points

If the number of Root Anchor Points (RAPs) is equal to the expected number of slots in a block, there will be a slot for every home address. This is desirable if synonyms are not expected to be a problem.

Increasing the number of RAPs tends to decrease the number of synonyms. If synonyms are expected, it is also better to have more slots than RAPS. (The number of slots is increased by increasing the block size and/or decreasing the byte limit.) In this way there are extra slots in a block to receive the possible synonyms, and to that extent the synonym chain can be searched without extra physical

I/Os. But this can also mean less dense packing of the RAA where synonyms are not encountered.

Having more RAPs than slots can be a disadvantage if all RAPs are used because some RAPs in one block will then have to point to home addresses in another block. This would require an additional (and unnecessary) physical I/O to access the required root.

Depending on the expectation of synonyms, the number of RAPs should be equal to or slightly less than the expected number of slots per block. However, if a significant number of records are expected to be short, the number of RAPs should be increased.

Byte Limit (Size of Slots)

Root Addressable Area slots should be large enough to hold the segments most likely to be accessed with the root. An alternate size criterion is that they be large enough to hold the average-sized database record. For slots larger than these criteria, there is an increased likelihood of transferring unneeded dependent segments into and out of main memory.

A larger byte limit without increasing the block size also means fewer slots within a block. This not only increases the chances for synonyms, it also increases the likelihood that the synonym chains will span blocks and thus require more I/Os when searched.

On the other hand, a smaller byte limit means more and smaller slots and will result in more root segments and fewer dependent segments being brought into main memory when a block is accessed. Because HDAM is based on the concept of accessing roots in a random sequence, there may not be a significant advantage in obtaining more roots in a given I/O operation. But there can certainly be a disadvantage in obtaining too few dependent segments.

Number of Blocks in Root Addressable Area

More blocks in the RAA mean more RAPs available for roots. This means a smaller likelihood of synonyms. Those roots that would have been synonyms (if there were fewer RAPs) can now be accessed more quickly. It also means less likelihood of filling the RAA and then having to place additional roots into the Overflow area. The less dense packing resulting from more RAA blocks is conducive to the future growth of the data base, and it means a greater likelihood that subsequent insertions can be made in favorable locations.

If the number of blocks and the byte limit are both increased in such a way that the number of slots remains constant, there can be more dependent segments per slot. The result here would be faster access to those additional dependent segments now included in the same slot as their root. A large number of blocks can have a negative impact if doing sequential processing in a HDAM data base.

To reduce the negative effects of synonyms, there should be enough blocks to provide slightly more slots than roots in the current data base plus its expected growth.

Size of the Overflow Area

The Overflow area is that portion of the data set left after the size of the RAA has been specified. Thus there is no DBD parameter for Overflow area size.

The primary consideration regarding the size of the Overflow area is to provide sufficient room for future growth of the data base. On the other hand, because a physical I/O is possible in accessing each Overflow area block, we would like to confine the majority of activity to segments in the RAA block for the record being processed. If the Overflow area fills too rapidly (and performance degrades as it fills), or is used too frequently, it may be desirable to increase the size of the RAA so that it can contain all of the more active segments.

Free Space

Free space is generally counterproductive in the Root Addressable Area of HDAM data bases. Since roots are randomly distributed throughout the RAA, slots that have not yet been filled constitute free space anyway, and they also are randomly distributed throughout the RAA. Specifying RAA free space in the DBD simply reduces the number of slots available to the randomizer algorithm, and this results in a higher likelihood that synonyms must be chained into other blocks. Free space in secondary data-set groups of a HDAM data base can be helpful.

DETERMINING HDAM PARAMETERS

The following procedure is recommended for determining a starting set of HDAM parameters. Bear in mind that these are intended merely as initial estimates. The best choices will depend on many factors, especially the use to which the data base will be put. Time estimates and modeling, as will be discussed in Chapter 17 and 18, are strongly recommended as ways of "tuning" these parameters *before* allocating and loading the data base.

A recommended method of determining initial HDAM parameter estimates is as follows:

1. Assign infrequently used segment types to secondary data-set groups.
2. Choose a RAA byte limit that will accommodate a root segment and enough dependent segments for the expected majority of accesses. In the absence of such criteria, a popular starting byte limit is the average record size plus 80 percent.
3. Estimate the number of records per block as the effective block size divided by the byte limit.
4. Estimate the number of RAPs per block as the expected number of records per block plus 0 to 20 percent. If most of the records are expected to exceed the byte limit, don't add the additional RAPs. But if many of the records may be shorter than the byte limit, then additional records (i.e., slots) per block are possible, and up to 20 percent more RAPs may be appropriate. If synonyms are expected, the number of RAPs might be decreased.
5. Establish the number of blocks in the RAA as the total number of expected records divided by the estimated number of records per block. Add 10 to 20 percent to this number to reduce the likelihood of synonyms.

5
HIERARCHICAL INDEXED DIRECT ACCESS
METHOD—HIDAM

DESCRIPTION

A HIDAM data base is composed of two separate data bases (Figure 5-1). All of the data resides in one data base while the other data base serves as the index. The index is implemented as a separate HISAM-like data base. Our discussion in this chapter will be limited to the main data base containing the data segments.

The HIDAM data base is organized into blocks (OSAM) or control intervals (VSAM) into which the data segments are stored. There are no logical records, no Root Addressable Area slots, and no Overflow area.

HIDAM STORAGE PATTERNS

The following sections demonstrate how segments are stored in a HIDAM data base. To illustrate these examples, the data-base records of Figure 5-2 will be used.

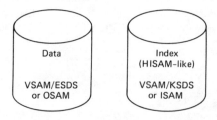

Figure 5-1. General organization of a HIDAM data base.

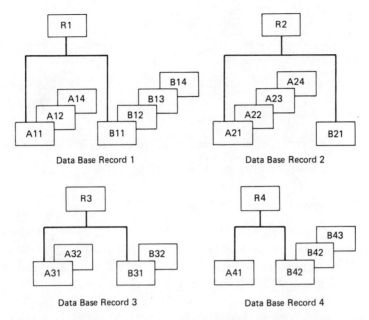

Figure 5-2. Data-base record examples.

Initial Loading

Root segment key values must be unique and should be loaded in sequence. Dependent segments must be loaded in hierarchical sequence behind their roots. Loading starts at the beginning of the data base, and the segments are placed physically one after the other. To accommodate expected growth of the data base, free space can be reserved at initial load time and at reorganization time. Free space within blocks and free blocks can both be specified as DBD parameters.

As each new root is encountered, an index entry is created for it. The root is then stored immediately after the segment that preceded it. A segment that cannot fit into the remaining space in a block will begin a new block. Figure 5-3 illustrates the initial loading of database records R1, R2, R3, and R4 from the structures depicted in Figure 5-2.

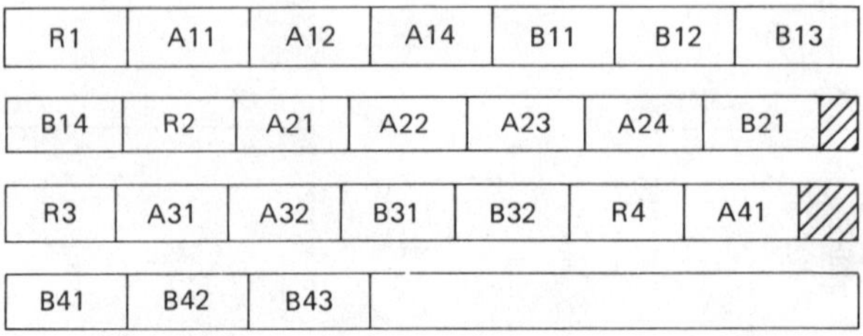

| R1 | A11 | A12 | A14 | B11 | B12 | B13 |

| B14 | R2 | A21 | A22 | A23 | A24 | B21 | ░ |

| R3 | A31 | A32 | B31 | B32 | R4 | A41 | ░ |

| B41 | B42 | B43 | |

Figure 5–3. Initial loading of data-base records R1, R2, R3, and R4.

Inserting Segments After Initial Load

For normal processing after initial load, HIDAM invokes a space search algorithm to determine where to place additional root and dependent segments. Details of this algorithm can be found in the IBM publication *IMS/VS Version 1 Data Base Administration Guide* (Ref. 7). For our purposes it is sufficient to say that HIDAM tries to place a root segment into the same block with the root having the next highest key, and it tries to place a dependent segment into the same block with its parent. Failing to find room in such a block, it next looks for a block that is already in the buffer pool so as to reduce the need for another physical I/O. Failing in this, it then selects a block in the storage device in such a way as to reduce expected future physical I/Os.

Deleting Segments

When segments are physically deleted, the gaps are not closed, and the space is made available for future inserts.

Replacing Segments

The replacement of fixed-length segments occurs in a very straightforward manner following their retrieval. Updated segments are simply returned to the places they occupied. Replacing variable-length segments becomes a problem if the segment has expanded. HIDAM must place expanded segments into a new location. Again, the vacated location is made available for future insertions.

HIDAM PERFORMANCE CHARACTERISTICS

HIDAM combines the benefits of sequential processing of root segments and selective processing of dependent segments. Its primary disadvantage is that time must be expended searching the index Thus at least one physical I/O for the index is required in addition to the physical I/O for the root segment. In addition, inserting and deleting HIDAM roots require corresponding updates of the index. By contrast, HDAM root segments are obtained in a single I/O, except when long synonym chains must be searched.

When doing sequential processing of HIDAM root segments, a significant time saving is possible by using physical twin forward pointers to go directly from root to root rather than by making a separate access to the index to locate the next root. Because of the architecture of DL/I, physical twin backward pointers must also be present in the root segments to implement this capability.

Summary of HIDAM Characteristics

1. The index may be reorganized without reorganizing the indexed data.
2. Space from deleted segments can be reused immediately.
3. Segments are not physically moved to make room for inserted segments.
4. A data base may be split into data set groups at any hierarchical level.

The major disadvantages of HIDAM are as follows:

1. Direct access to a root segment may be slower than with HDAM because the index must be accessed.
2. Additional storage space is required for the index data base.

SUMMARY OF HIDAM DESIGN PARAMETERS

In this section we will review the design parameters directly associated with HIDAM and discuss the performance implications of each. Even here, the number of interrelationships and trade-offs causes us to give general considerations rather than concrete choices. We will discuss the CI and free space.

CI (Block) Size

If doing key-sequence processing of roots, HIDAM blocks should normally be as long as buffer sizes and physical device characteristics permit. Shorter blocks mean more blocks, and thus more physical I/Os are required to access the same number of records and segments. This guideline is based on the concept of more than one complete data-base record per block, as is the case in HIDAM.

For random processing of roots, one data-base record per block, if attainable, is the ideal. Here, a block size equal to average record size is preferable. This guideline has most meaning when the data-base records are of equal or nearly equal length.

In both cases we assume that data-base records are shortened and made more nearly equal in length by relegating infrequently used segment types to separate data set groups (see Chapter 8).

Free Space

Free space in HIDAM data bases is used to provide for inserting root segments into physical locations that correspond as nearly as possible with root key sequence, and for inserting dependents into blocks as nearly as possible according to their hierarchical sequence. This serves to reduce the number of physical I/Os between blocks that will be required later when accessing these inserted segments.

In this regard, free space within blocks is more important than free blocks. Both types of free space also enhance the capability of future data-base expansion. If the number of future insertions is known and if they are expected to be evenly distributed, then free space within blocks is all that is needed. Otherwise, free blocks are also useful.

Too much free space can be expensive. Not only is unused storage space implied, but free space within blocks means fewer segments per block. This can have a negative performance impact by requiring physical I/Os to more blocks to access the same number of segments.

Free space within blocks is usually estimated at 5–20% of effective block size. Initial estimates of free blocks usually range from every fifth block to every 20th block.

6
ACCESS METHOD SELECTION CRITERIA

SELECTION CRITERIA

Having presented the characteristics of the basic DL/I access methods, we can now formulate some rules and guidelines for selecting the access method most appropriate for a given situation. The selection criteria can be presented in a very simple or in a rather complex format. We will begin with the simple.

Basic Selection Criteria

HISAM is appropriate for a nonvolatile data base in which dependent segments are processed in a predominately sequential manner. Otherwise, if the data base is volatile or if dependent segment processing is not sequential, one of the HD access methods is usually more appropriate. Of the HD methods, HIDAM is usually preferred when sequential precessing of the root segments is important or when HDAM synonyms might be a problem. On the other hand, HDAM is usually preferred for random selection of root segments, because by avoiding an index search it usually finds a root segment faster than does HIDAM.

A concise access-method selection criteria, therefore, can be stated as follows:

- If the data base is nonvolatile and dependent segment processing is sequential, use HISAM.
- Otherwise, if root segment processing is sequential or if collisions may be a problem, use HIDAM.
- Otherwise, use HDAM.

Guide Selection Criteria

A more detailed and comprehensive access method selection criteria was prepared by the Information Management Group of the GUIDE International Corporation. This criteria is in the form of a decision table published in *The Data Base Design Guide* in 1974 (Reference 3).

The top portion of the decision table (Figure 6–1) represents the considerations pertinent to access method selection. For each consideration (row), a blank column represents either a "no" or "don't care" condition, whereas a Y represents a "yes" condition. The Ys further represent either the only characteristic or the most important or overriding characteristic.

The rows of the bottom portion of the table represent the suggested choices. For a given column selected by responses to the considerations, an X in that column suggests a choice to be considered.

ON ACCESSING THE ROOT SEGMENT

A revealing comparison of the HDAM, HIDAM, and HISAM access methods from a performance standpoint is to observe the work required in accessing their root segments. The steps involved to access HDAM data-base roots are the following:

- Randomize the key.
- Access the root segment.   (1 to 1.2 I/Os)

To access a root segment in a HIDAM data base requires the following steps:

- Access the VSAM index set.
- Access the VSAM sequence set.
- Access the HIDAM index.
- Access the root segment.   (Up to 4 I/Os)

Finally, to access a root segment in a HISAM data base requires the following steps:

All accessing is batch seq; high activity on file	YYYYY			
Or processing largely seq; some individual query		YYYYYYYYY		
Only file maint. is seq; high activity is update			YYYYYYYYYYYY	
Or partly seq; high query and trans. activity				YYYYYYYYYYYYY
And has a future potential as a data base	Y	Y	Y	Y
Has a high degree of redundant data across files	YY	Y	Y	Y
Data fields added, descriptions changed frequently	Y	Y	Y	Y
Need to access data on a variety of different keys		Y	Y	Y
Need fast response or low volume, unpredictable incidence of queries		Y	Y Y Y Y	Y Y Y Y
Need relationships between segs of the same data base		Y	YY	YY
Need relationships among several data bases		Y	YY	YY
Need high activity on a portion of the data base, low activity on the remainder	Y	Y	YY	YY
Traditional Sequential	X X		X	
HSAM	X X X	X	X X	
HISAM	XX	X	X	
HDAM			X X X X	X X X X
HIDAM		XXXXX	X X.X X XX	XXX X X X
And Physical Pointers		XX	XXXX	XXX X
Logical Pointers		X	XX	XX
Multiple Data Set Groups	X		X	XX	XX

Figure 6-1. Data-base organization decision table.

- Access the VSAM index set.
- Access the VSAM sequence set.
- Access the root segment.   (Up to 3 I/Os)

ACCESS METHOD GUIDELINES

Having selected a DL/I access method, various options are available for its physical implementation. The following physical design guidelines are offered to assist the designer with the physical design choices.

HISAM

- HISAM data bases are fast loading, provide for good sequential processing, and the I/O time for random access to root segments can be nearly as fast as HDAM.
- HISAM performs well for nonvolatile, fixed-length data bases requiring sequential processing of whole data-base records.
- Use VSAM for HISAM data bases to eliminate chains on roots inserted after initial load and to provide free space for logical records inserted after initial load.

HD General

- Use physical child/physical twin pointers unless all segments in the subtree are to be accessed sequentially.
- Specify twin backward pointers on segments subject to frequent deletions to improve deletion performance.
- Free space within a block should be large enough for the largest segment type.
- The first occurrence of a HDAM or HIDAM segment type located in a secondary data set group has no favored block for insertion after initial load.

HDAM

- Avoid specifying twin backward pointers for HDAM roots. They require space and they must be maintained when inserting and deleting segments. They have value only when deleting segments in which key sequence among twins is important, and this is not the case with HDAM roots.
- GET NEXT processing at the root level in HDAM proceeds in physical RAP sequence with synonyms maintained in logical key sequence of their RAP.
- To access HDAM root segments sequentially, consider (1) using

a secondary index for limited use, (2) using a randomizing routine that assigns RAPs in logical sequence, or (3) retrieving the roots in RAP sequence and sorting the result.
- Specifying HDAM free space is self-defeating except in secondary data set groups.

HIDAM

- In the DBD, specify PTR = TB (twin backward) or NONE for the root segment. This will avoid the allocation and maintenance of a RAP in each block. It also permits faster sequential access for one root to the next via the twin forward pointer rather than by referencing the index for each root. Finally, without the twin backward pointer, the twin forward pointers are not maintained as roots are inserted or deleted.
- GET NEXT processing at the root level in HIDAM avoids accessing the index by proceeding along the physical twin chain if twin backward pointers are specified.
- A GET NEXT call to a root with key qualification always proceeds via the index if the call cannot be satisfied at the current position.
- Use VSAM for the HIDAM primary index to eliminate the OSAM overflow data set.
- For insert activity against a HIDAM data base, specify free space in the DBD.

VSAM ESDS VS. OSAM

The VSAM Entry Sequenced Access Method (VSAM ESDS) and the Overflow Sequential Access Method (OSAM) are both candidates as the operating system access method for supporting the HDAM and the HIDAM data bases. OSAM is generally considered to be the faster of the two for the following reasons:

- OSAM searches the buffer pool more efficiently by trying adjacent buffers before going to the Least Recently Used (LRU) chain.

- With OSAM, buffer subpools can be selectively page fixed rather than page fixing the entire buffer pool.
- OSAM locates buffers by hashing rather than by chaining.
- OSAM permits more possible block sizes than VSAM.
- OSAM permits the use of multiple subpools of the same size.
- Aside from the above considerations, OSAM has a shorter path length—that is, it requires the execution of fewer CPU instructions.

PART III
PERFORMANCE ASPECTS OF
PHYSICAL DESIGN OPTIONS

7
BLOCK SIZES

INTRODUCTION

The selection of block size is one of the more critical design choices from the performance standpoint. A block is the unit of information transferred across the channel between main memory and the storage device when a physical I/O occurs. For data bases using VSAM, the block is called a *control interval*. A block generally contains several segments. Minimizing the number of blocks transferred can have a significant effect on I/O time and thus on response time. The proper choice of block size depends heavily on the access method used and on the type of processing to be done. Block sizes will be discussed for each of the four major DL/I access methods, but first some general comments are in order.

GENERAL COMMENTS

Generally speaking, we want to minimize the number of blocks read into the buffer pools for an application. This means selecting a block size and organizing the block contents so that we maximize the amount of useful information in each block that is read in.

Minimum block size is easy to determine. A block must be at least as long as the longest segment it is to contain. Maximum block size is more elusive. General guidelines frequently say that a block should be no longer than the longest data base record. This general guideline is based on the premise that one I/O (rather than more than one) is ideal for a single data base record, and that there will be no more than one record per block. On this assumption, blocks longer than the longest record will certainly contain empty waste space. But this does not apply when we have portions of several records in the same block, as is frequently the case. Therefore we shall talk of *optimum* rather than *maximum* block size. Figure 7-1 depicts the generalized criteria for minimum block size.

As we shall see, optimum block size is sometimes the longest block possible, and at other times is based on record length. For example, if the more frequently used applications do not process all the segment types in a record, it may be advantageous to have only portions of the entire record in a block. On the other hand, if the processing is predominately record after record in root key sequence, it may be advantageous to have portions of more than one record in a block.

The guidelines for determining block size depend on the access method used. Therefore, in focusing on guidelines for optimum block size (i.e., for blocks that contain a maximum of useful information), each major DL/I access method will be considered separately. But first, it will be helpful to review considerations for the way space is used within the blocks.

Space Considerations

The number of actual data bytes that can be stored in a block will be somewhat less than the block size. In addition to the segments themselves, some portion of each block is occupied by overhead information, free space, and waste space. Thus we speak of *effective block size* when referring to the amount of data that can be stored in a block. (See Chapter 18 for the calculation of effective block size.)

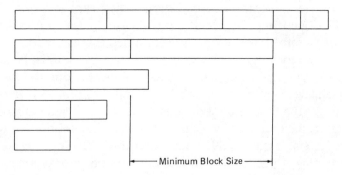

Figure 7-1. Minimum block size.

Depending on the access method used, the block overhead information can contain items such as Free Space Elements (FSEs), Root Anchor Points (RAPs), Control Interval Definition Fields (CIDFs), Record Definition Fields (RDFs), and Overflow Pointers.

In addition to the block overhead, each segment carries its own overhead. Each segment is divided into a data portion and a prefix portion. The prefix contains pointers and indicative information.

Free space and waste space will be explained more fully in the following subsections.

Interrecord gaps are a further consideration. The size of the VSAM interrecord gaps varies with the speed of the various disk devices. Small block sizes can cause poor space utilization because of relatively larger and more frequent interrecord gaps.

Free Space. Free space has meaning when loading or reorganizing the data base. It is a measure of the amount of space to be left empty during the loading or reorganizing process. There are two kinds of free space. *Free Space Within Blocks (FSW)* is the amount of segment space within each block to remain empty at load time. *Free Space Between Blocks (FSB)* specifies the number of blocks to remain completely empty of segments at load time. The purpose of free space is to provide for data-base growth as additional segments are inserted during processing, and the amounts of free space to be reserved are specified in the DBD.

The concept of free space is depicted in Figure 7-2.

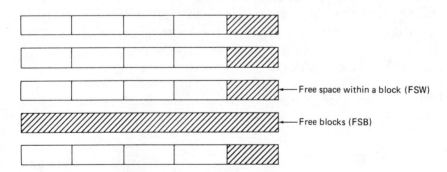

Figure 7-2. The concept of free space.

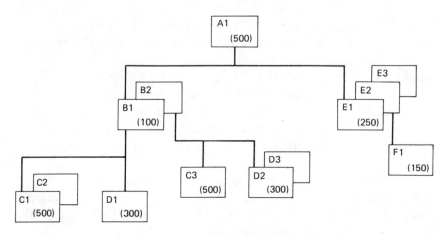

Figure 7-3. Example data-base record A1.

Waste Space.   Waste space is that space (outside the realm of free space and interrecord gaps) that remains empty at load time. It can be termed *unintentional empty space*. Although this space is available for future updates, it is an undesirable way of providing expansion capability. Free space is the preferred way of accommodating expansion. The ideal is to have no waste space. Figures 7-3 and 7-4 illustrate a data-base record that fits exactly into two 2K blocks with no waste space.

There are two kinds of waste space. The first kind of waste space is the space left at the end of a block (or logical record) when the next segment to be loaded will not fit. The second kind of waste space is the space at the end of a block (or logical record) after the last segment of a data-base record when the next root is required to go into a new block (or logical record). Figures 7-5 and 7-6 illustrate the two kinds of waste space.

HSAM and HIDAM will have only the first kind of waste space. With both of these access methods, each new root segment goes into the same block (if it will fit) as the last segment of the previous record.

A1	B1	C1	C2	D1	B2		C3	D2	D3	E1	E2	F1	E3
500	100	500	500	300	100		500	300	300	250	250	150	250

Figure 7-4. Record A1 contained in two 2K blocks (no waste space).

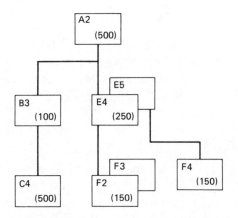

Figure 7–5. Example data-base record A2.

In HISAM, blocks in the primary data set are divided evenly into logical records, with a root and as many dependent segments as will fit going into each logical record. The remaining segments go into the overflow data set, which is also divided into logical records. The overflow segments for a data-base record start in a new overflow logical record; they do not start in the remaining empty space of a logical record that has already been partially filled. Thus waste space in HISAM is on a logical record basis rather than on a block basis. Logical records in both the primary data set and the overflow data set are subject to waste space of both kinds.

In HDAM, blocks in the Root Addressable Area are divided into slots of varying but maximum size, but blocks in the Overflow area are not subdivided. With regard to space requirements, the HDAM slots are different from the HISAM logical records. Each HDAM slot can contain a root segment and as many dependent segments as will fit, but the next root goes immediately thereafter. The remaining segments of each data-base record go into the Overflow area starting in the same block (if sufficient space exists) as the last segment from the previous record. Hence, waste space in HDAM is entirely of the first kind.

A2	B3	C4	E4	F2	F3	E5	Waste
500	100	500	250	150	150	250	100

F4	Waste
150	1850

Figure 7–6. Record A2 contained in two 2K blocks (two kinds of waste space).

ACCESS METHOD CONSIDERATIONS

In all cases below, except HSAM, it will be assumed that infrequently used segment types are separated into secondary data set groups. Thus, "average" record size will refer to the segment types remaining in the primary data set group.

Block Sizes for HSAM

The idea behind HSAM is the sequential processing of every segment of each record in the data base. Accessing always begins with the root of the first data-base record, and it proceeds sequentially from that point. The segments are physically stored in strict hierarchical sequence. Therefore, the more segments that can be brought in with each physical I/O, the fewer I/Os will have to be performed to access all the segments.

Maximum I/O efficiency is obtained by having blocks as long as possible. Thus with HSAM block size is limited only by the constraints of the storage device and/or the buffer pools.

Block Sizes for HISAM

In HISAM, block size is a less critical parameter than logical record length, which is discussed in Chapter 3. Assuming sequential processing of the data-base records and their segments (for which HISAM is designed) as opposed to random access to the records, HISAM block size should be as large as possible consistent with acceptable paging rates and physical device constraints. This general rule holds for update environments as well as read environments.

Block Sizes for HDAM

Determining optimum block sizes for HDAM data bases is more difficult and elusive than in the cases of HSAM or HISAM. Here we assume that because of random access, each data-base record is equally likely to be the next one accessed. So now the question becomes one of the maximizing the likelihood that the next record to be accessed is already in memory in the buffer pool. This likelihood is maximized by maximizing the number of records that can be contained in the buffer pool. The number of records that can be contained in the buffer pool is determined by the block size (which identifies a certain subpool) and the number of buffers in that subpool. The size of the subpool is equal to the product of subpool buffer size times the number of buffers in the subpool. We will assume a fixed subpool size chosen as large as possible consistent with acceptable paging activity. Thus we can have smaller blocks and more buffers or larger blocks and fewer buffers.

Larger blocks mean more transfer time, and they bring in (assuming several records or slots per block) extra information that is no more likely to be wanted next than the information already in the buffer pool. On the other hand, shorter blocks mean more initial physical I/O activity until the buffer pool becomes filled. The issue is further complicated by the fact that the number of records that can be represented in a HDAM block is variable, and is closely related to other variables such as byte limit, number of RAPs, and number of synonyms.

The actual determination of optimum block size is best done by simulation or modeling (see Chapter 20). However, some guidelines can be offered for a starting estimate. The criteria for block size given below, suggested by Jack McElreath (Reference 11), serve well for providing a starting point. The following guidelines are suggested:

1. Select a byte limit for the average data-base-record size.
2. Select the starting block size according to the following criteria:
   - If the average data-base-record size is under 500 characters, use a 2K block size.
   - If the average data-base-record size is 500 to 4000 characters, use a 4K block size.
   - If over 4000 characters, use a block large enough to hold one average data-base record. (Remember with VSAM we are restricted to 2K, 4K, 8K, 12K, and 16K.)
3. Once block size and byte limit are selected, the expected number of slots is determined. Specify the number of RAPs to be close to, or slightly greater than, the number of slots. If synonyms are expected to be a problem, slightly reduce the number of RAPs.

Block Sizes for HIDAM

HIDAM differs from HDAM in two major respects. Because the HIDAM root segments are indexed, HIDAM lends itself both to sequential and random processing of root segments. In addition, HIDAM has no overflow area, and all segments of a data-base record are loaded in physically adjacent positions in hierarchical sequence, with the root of the next record being placed immediately after the last segment of the previous record. Thus there could be more than one record in a block. On the other hand, a long data-base record could be split over one or more blocks. Even though the roots are in physical key sequence when the data base is loaded, random processing of the roots means that the next root block is no more likely to be the next one wanted than any other root. In this case, one average record per block seems to be ideal, and the optimum block size could be based on the criteria given above for HDAM.

The more common situation with HIDAM is that sequential processing of roots is desired. Because the roots are loaded and physically stored in key sequence order, the next root in the block is likely to be the next root wanted, and the block size should be as large as possible.

In either case, if frequent insertions and deletions of root segments occur, the physical ordering of root segments by key value begins to deteriorate, and the I/O savings from having several roots in the same block begins to diminish. In the extreme, the remedy is block sizes again based on average record length, or more frequent reorganizations.

8
DATA SET GROUPS

DEFINITION

A DL/I data base can be loaded into more than one data set, with each data set containing all occurrences of one or more segment types. These data sets are called *data set groups*. The data set group containing occurrences of the root segment is called the *primary* data set group. The other data set groups for the same data base are called *secondary* data set groups.

Each data set group is implemented as a separate data set identified to the operating system by its own DD statement. DL/I treats these separate data set groups as one data base, and the accessing logic within an application program remains the same.

To illustrate the concept of data set groups, consider a data base having the logical design illustrated in Figure 8-1.

Arbitrarily (for now), let's divide this data base into three data set groups so that segment types of equal size are grouped together. We

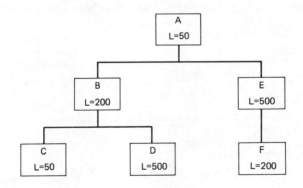

Figure 8-1. A data-base record.

can assign segment types A and C (50 bytes) to one group, segment types B and F (200 bytes) to another group, and segment types D and E (500 bytes) to the third group. We now have three data sets containing all occurrences of their assigned segment types, as shown in Figure 8-2, with all segments of each data set group being of equal length.

In this example, the data set containing the occurrences of segment A (the root segment) will be the primary data set group. The other two are secondary data set groups.

REASONS FOR DATA SET GROUPS

Data set groups offer several advantages with regard to space utilization and processing efficiency. But if used unwisely, they can also present some disadvantages. As we explore the various data set group considerations, the data-base designer should keep in mind that in a real design study, several of these considerations may be present, and the choices will depend on appropriate trade-offs. Hopefully, an understanding of the individual considerations will help the designer make the best choices according to the situation at hand.

We will now discuss considerations of space conservation, free space variations, accessing efficiency, and off-line storage.

Space Conservation

A frequent reason for using data set groups is space conservation. By grouping segment types of like (or almost like) size together, significant reductions of waste space are possible. This concept was il-

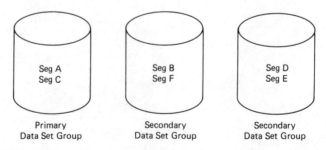

Figure 8-2. Three data set groups.

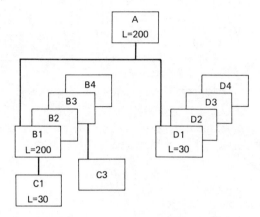

Figure 8–3. A data-base record.

lustrated in a general manner in the introductory section. For a more explicit example, consider the data-base record depicted in Figure 8-3, and suppose we are loading the segments (in hierarchical order) into blocks of 1000 bytes (effective storage). The storage pattern of Figure 8-4 will emerge.

In this example, we see 140 bytes of waste space in the first block because the next segment, B4, will not fit. In the second block we see the second kind of waste space (650 bytes), which exists because there are no more segments to be loaded for this data-base record. Of course, all this waste space is available for inserts during processing, but at best some space will remain wasted when segments to be inserted are larger than the space available. This is always a potential problem when grouping segments of significantly different lengths together.

On the other hand, by using two data set groups with blocks having effective lengths of 1000 and 1800, respectively, we can assign segment types A and B to one data set group and segment types C

A	B1	C1	B2	B3	C3	Waste
200	200	30	200	200	30	140

B4	D1	D2	D3	D4	D5	Waste
200	30	30	30	30	30	650

Figure 8–4. Two blocks in one data set group.

A	B1	B2	B3	B4
200	200	200	200	200

(a)

Figure 8–5a. Primary data set group (block size = 1000).

and D to the other data set group, with no waste of space at all when the blocks are filled. This assignment situation is shown in Figure 8–5.

Free Space Variations

Contrary to the space conservation principle discussed above, it is sometimes advantageous to accept a space inefficiency in order to gain other benefits. Suppose that in a certain data base, some segment types are subject to frequent insertions and deletions while other segment types are relatively stable. Because each data set group is implemented as a separate data set, each group can have its own space parameters. Thus the stable segments can be tightly packed into one data set group while the more volatile segments can be loosely packed into one or more other data set groups. This is a way of conserving space for the stable segments while accomodating the less dense packing required for efficient insertions and for growth with regard to the volatile segments.

Accessing Efficiency

Data set groups offer the potential for significant performance improvements. The following example will illustrate this possibility. Consider a data base structured as shown in Figure 8–6, with a typical data-base record in Figure 8–7.

Suppose further that the physical design calls for no secondary

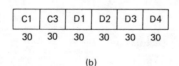

C1	C3	D1	D2	D3	D4
30	30	30	30	30	30

(b)

Figure 8–5b. Secondary data set group (block size = 2100).

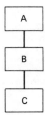

Figure 8–6. A data-base structure.

data set groups and that the segments are blocked as shown in Figure 8–8.

Now suppose that an application function accesses root A and all type B segments but not the type C segments. To access root A and the type B segments shown in Figure 8–8, both blocks will have to be accessed requiring two physical I/Os. But consider two data set groups (Figure 8–9) organized so that all the type B segments are in the primary data set group with the root while the type C segments are separated into a secondary data set group. In this case, the required type B segments are in one block with their root and can be accessed with a single I/O.

But a performance degradation is also possible if the grouping is inconsistent with the needs of the program. To illustrate the detrimental effect on performance that is possible, consider the same grouping as depicted in Figure 8–9, but now assume a different application function that accesses the root segment A, and then ac-

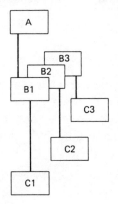

Figure 8–7. A data-base record.

A	B1	C1	B2

C2	B3	C3	

Figure 8–8. One data set group, two blocks.

cesses the type B and C segments in pairs—that is, B1, C1, B2, C2,
B3, and C3. At worst, assuming only one of these blocks can reside
in the buffer pool, we would require six physical I/Os in ping-pong-
ing back and forth between the block of Bs and the block of Cs. At
best, assuming both blocks can be read but can remain in the buffer
pools, two I/Os would be required. For this example, the blocking
in a single data set (Figure 8-8) will yield more favorable performance.

Frequently, processing efficiency and space conservation are joint
considerations. Consider the situation of a data base in which 90
percent of the records are short and 10 percent are relatively long,
and suppose that 90 percent of the activity is against the long records. It would be tempting to use long logical records (HISAM) or
long RAA slots (HDAM) to reduce activity in the overflow areas for
the activity against the long records. In HISAM this would result in
many partially empty logical records holding the short records. In
HDAM it would mean fewer RAPs and slots per block which in turn
would imply empty space in some blocks. Data set groups are a way
of separating out unneeded segment types and having effective record
lengths that are more equal in the HISAM logical records or the
HDAM slots.

Off-Line Storage

Another reason for using data set groups is to reduce on-line storage
requirements. Only those secondary groups required for a given application scheduling need be on-line. Thus for a billing function, cus-
tomer billing information could be divided into four secondary data

Figure 8–9. A primary and a secondary data set group, one block in each.

set groups. One group could be mounted for billing the first week of a month, another group could be mounted for billing the second week of the month, and so on. In this way the on-line storage requirement could be reduced by approximately 75 percent.

RULES FOR ESTABLISHING DATA SET GROUPS

The rules for determining which segment types can go into which data set groups depend on the access method being used. HSAM data bases cannot be divided into data set groups. For HISAM, the rules for establishing data set groups are as follows:

- Up to nine secondary data set groups are permitted.
- The root segment must be in the primary group.
- A secondary data set group must begin with a second-level dependent of the root and must contain all of its dependent segments.
- Each data set group (primary and secondary) must contain all segment types, in hierarchical order, up to the second-level segment type that begins the next group.
- Data set groups are not supported for VSAM.
- Data set groups are not supported for secondary indexing.

For HDAM and HIDAM, the following rules apply:

- Up to nine secondary data set groups are permitted.
- The root segment must be in the primary group.
- Any combination of other segment types can be in any group.
- If a physical parent is in a different group from its physical children, they must be connected by physical child/physical twin pointers rather than by hierarchic pointers.

SUMMARIZING GUIDELINES

This section summarizes the main guidelines presented in this chapter.

- A space saving can usually be obtained by placing segments of equal (or nearly equal) length together into one data set group, and by assigning segments of other similar lengths to other data set groups.

- Try to avoid grouping segments of widely varying lengths into a single secondary data set group. Since the bit map only keeps track of blocks having enough space for the largest segment type, it sometimes happens that smaller segments cannot be inserted even though adequate room for them exists.

- By separating segments of high insertion/deletion activity into a separate data set group, block size and free space parameters can be chosen to give adequate room for expected expansion, while the other data set groups (containing less volatile segment types) can have different block sizes and free space parameters for a more dense packing of segments.

- When doing little or no inserting a performance advantage is possible by separating frequently and infrequently used segments into separate data set groups. This allows the frequently used segments to be packed more densely into the same block than would otherwise be possible.

- An ideal situation is when all of the data-base records (or at least the most active portions) are the same size. Then block size can be selected to contain the entire record (or the active portion thereof). If unequal record sizes are caused by the presence or absence of certain segment types, consider separating these segment types into one or more secondary data set groups.

- If using data set groups for space conservation, suppose the root and a third-level segment type are in the same group. If the second-level segment type is of a different size, placing it into a separate data set group could create a performance disadvantage because of the possible extra physical I/Os in going from the first data set group to the second and then back to the first.

- In a HISAM data base, an index is established to the second-level segments that are used to begin secondary data set groups. This provides a potential performance advantage because access can be made directly to these second-level segments without going through the root. In effect, each secondary data set group becomes a HISAM sub data base.

- When using secondary data set groups, design the application program call patterns in such a way as to minimize any accessing back and forth between the data set groups.

9
LOGICAL RELATIONS

INTRODUCTION

Consider the two physical data bases shown in Figure 9-1. One data base begins with SKILL as its root segment, and the other begins with NAME as its root segment and has SKILL as a child of NAME. At this point we will not concern ourselves with why two separate data bases are desired. The important thing is that there are two different sets of the same SKILL segments, one set in each data base. We want to eliminate this redundancy, and we can do so through logical relations.

The discussion in this chapter will deal only with the functional characteristics of logical relations. In Chapter 11 the mechanics of implementing logical relations will be presented. The terms *physical parent, physical child, logical parent,* and *logical child* were defined in Chapter 1.

First we will discuss logical relations in general, and then we will describe the three types of logical relations:

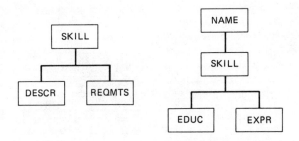

Figure 9-1. Two physical data bases.

- Unidirectional logical relations.
- Bidirectional logical relations with physical pairing.
- Bidirectional logical relations with virtual pairing.

LOGICAL RELATIONS IN GENERAL

As explained in Chapter 1, redundancy from multiple sets of the same segment type can be eliminated by designating one of the sets to contain the segment data and by using pointers in the segment occurrences in the other sets to point to the appropriate data segments. In the example we are using, we are eliminating redundancy of SKILL data that otherwise would exist in the SKILL and NAME data bases. For clarity, we will refer to the SKILL segments in the SKILL data base as SKILL1 and to the SKILL segments in the NAME data base as SKILL2. We will retain the data in the SKILL1 segments, and we will remove the data from the SKILL2 segments and provide SKILL2 pointers to the corresponding SKILL1 segments. Figure 9–2 depicts this organization.

Two types of pointers may be used: direct or symbolic. Direct pointers are four-byte addresses of the physical locations of the "target" segments. Symbolic pointers are the concatenated keys of the target segments. The concatenated keys define the access path to the target segment from its root. These pointers will be discussed in detail in Chapter 11.

By means of logical relations, an application program can be designed to process a *logical data base*, which is a logical view that results when physical data bases are connected with logical relations.

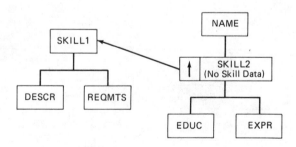

Figure 9–2. A logical relation.

Without going into the rules for deriving logical views for logically related data bases, the example at hand, starting with NAME as the root to be accessed, yields the logical view shown in Figure 9–3. While SKILL1 and SKILL2 segments both physically exist, as data and pointer segments respectively, the logical view shows only one SKILL segment type because there is only one set of skill data. The children EDUC and EXPR of SKILL2 are available as children of SKILL. The children DESCR and REQMTS of SKILL1 are also available as children of SKILL.

We need to go one step further. In eliminating redundancy, we removed the skill data from the SKILL2 segments. The empty SKILL2 segments are an ideal place to store a different kind of information that we call *intersection data*. Intersection data pertains to, and relates, a given physical parent occurrence and a given logical parent occurrence. Suppose, for example, that we want to store information pertaining to a given person and a given skill. Perhaps we will store each person's rating in each of his or her skills. The SKILL1 segments would not be a good place to store the rating, because there may be several people with the same skill, and we would have to store a variable number of ratings in a given SKILL1 segment. Similarly, the NAME segment would not be a good place because there can be many skills for each name. But for each name and related skill there is a unique SKILL2 segment relating them and which effectively forms an intersection between the two. The SKILL2 segments (in this case) are referred to as *intersection segments* as well as pointer segments, and they are ideally suited for intersection data. The SKILL1 segments, in this case, can also be referred to as *des-*

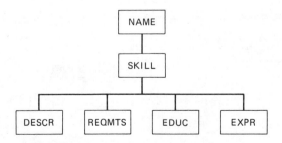

Figure 9–3. A logical data base.

tination parents. For now we will define destination parents as the logical parents that are the targets of the logical relation pointers in the pointer (or intersection) segments. In the section on virtual pairing, we will give an expanded definition of destination parents.

In the discussion to follow, intersection segments may be referred to as logical children or as physical children, depending on the perspective. Referring to Figure 9-2, we see that the intersection segments SKILL2 are logical children of SKILL1 (the logical parents), and at the same time they are physical children of NAME (the physical parents). The intersection segment has previously been referred to as a pointer segment. It is more commonly referred to as a logical child segment. The term to be used will depend on the nature and perspective of the discussion.

When IMS accesses a SKILL for a given NAME, IMS can return to the application program a composite segment made up of the contents of SKILL1 (destination parent) and SKILL2 (intersection segment). This type of result is depicted in Figure 9-4.

The exact contents of this composite segment can vary according to criteria specified in the DBD being used. Three alternatives are available: (1) concatenated key of destination parent, intersection data, and destination parent data; (2) concatenated key of destination parent and intersection data; or (3) destination parent data only.

Note that in cases 1 and 3 the destination parent must be accessed. It may or may not be accessed in case 2, depending on whether physical or virtual pairing is used, as will be explained in a later section.

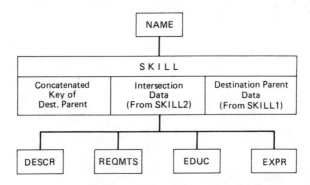

Figure 9-4. A logical data base.

TYPES OF LOGICAL RELATIONS

Unidirectional Logical Relations

The discussion thus far has pertained to traversal in one direction across a logical boundary. Unidirectional logical relations provide the ability to go in one direction, from a physical parent to a related set of logical parent occurrences. In our example, we have started with a NAME, with the intent of finding all the SKILLs recorded for that NAME. This can be contrasted with bidirectional logical relations, which provide the ability to go in either direction. Figure 9–2 depicts the unidirectional logical relation.

Bidirectional Logical Relations

Bidirectional logical relations provide for traversal in both directions. In one direction, for a given NAME one can find the associated SKILLs. In the other direction, for a given SKILL one can find the associated NAMEs.

Bidirectional logical relations offer two logical views of the constituent physical data bases. One view begins from the root of the physical parent; the other view begins from the root of the logical parent. For the example at hand, the resulting logical data bases are depicted in Figure 9–5.

Bidirectional—Physical Pairing.   Bidirectional logical relations with physical pairing (Figure 9–6) give the appearance of being a con-

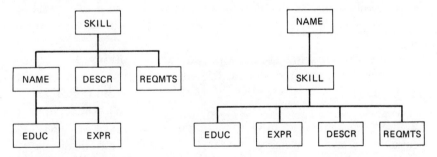

Figure 9–5. Logical data bases resulting from logical relations between SKILL and NAME.

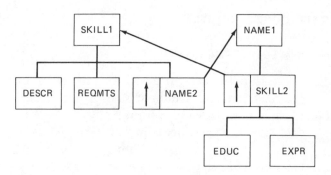

Figure 9-6. A bidirectional logical relation with physical pairing.

trolled form of using two unidirectional logical relations, one in each direction. The fundamental difference, however, is that bidirectional logical relations provide two-way traversal over a *single* relationship rather than over two different relationships.

Physical pairing means that there are two sets of logical child segments, one set for each direction of travel. For the example at hand, the SKILL2 segments under NAME1 will be used to find all SKILLs for each given NAME, and the NAME2 segments under SKILL1 will be used to find all NAMES for each given SKILL. Further, physical pairing implies a one-to-one correspondence between segment occurrences in each set of logical children. For example, for a given NAME and a given associated SKILL, a SKILL2 segment points from that NAME to that SKILL, and a corresponding NAME2 segment points in the opposite direction from the same SKILL to the same NAME. A third characteristic of physical pairing is that if a logical child segment in one set has intersection data, the same intersection data is in the corresponding logical child segment in the other set.

Physical pairing has significant update implications. If a logical child segment is inserted into or deleted from one set, a corresponding logical child must be inserted into or deleted from the other set. In addition, if the intersection data in one logical child segment is updated, the same update must be made to the other associated logical child. These "duplicate" updates are made automatically by the data base management system (IMS) and not by the application programmer, but they can be costly in terms of time.

Bidirectional—Virtual Pairing.   Virtual pairing is an alternative to physical pairing. Virtual pairing is a way of providing bidirectional capability with only one set of logical child segments (see Figure 9-7). The primary advantage of virtual pairing is that the double update characteristic of physically paired logical children is avoided, but at a lesser expense of maintaining (for insert and delete activity) additional pointers used to implement virtual pairing. Also, because there is only one set of logical children, virtual pairing requires less storage space than physical pairing.

With virtual pairing, traversal from physical parent to logical parent works just like unidirectional and physically paired bidirectional logical relations. But traversal from logical parent to physical parent must be implemented by additional pointers in the prefixes of the existing logical parent and logical child segments. (See Chapter 11 for implementation details.)

In virtual pairing, the term, *destination parent* needs further explanation. A destination parent is always the target, or destination, of the access. When traversing from physical parent through physical child (intersection segment) to logical parent, the destination parent is the logical parent. But when traversing from a logical parent through logical child (the same intersection segment) to physical parent, the destination parent is the physical parent. In addition, the concatenated key of the destination parent is one of the items returned to the application program. The concatenated key of the logical parent is contained in the intersection segment, but the

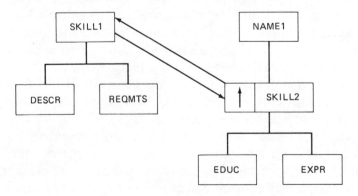

Figure 9-7. A bidirectional logical relation with virtual pairing.

concatenated key of the physical parent, when needed, must be dynamically constructed.

Double Unidirectional Logical Relations.   Two or more unidirectional logical relations can be used to traverse in opposite directions between the same physical and logical parents, and this implementation should be used if the relationships in the two directions are asynchronous (i.e., independent of one another). For example, suppose that for each SKILL we want to access the names of the people *having* that skill. On the other hand, for each NAME, we want to access the skills that each person *would like to obtain*. The relationships, "having" and "would like to obtain" are different (i.e., asynchronous) relationships, and an update to one relationship does not require a similar (i.e., paired) update to the other relationship. Therefore, bidirectional logical relations with either kind of pairing would be inappropriate for such situations.

PERFORMANCE IMPLICATIONS
OF LOGICAL RELATIONS

Space and Integrity Implications

Logical relations provide paths to segments from a parent other than the physical parent without requiring the duplication of those segments under the other parent. One benefit is that storage space is saved by not storing duplicate sets of the same segment types.

Much more importantly, data-base integrity is enhanced because of not having multiple copies of the same information to update when changes occur. When an update is made to one item of redundant data, it must also be made to all the duplicate items if they are to maintain consistency in their values. It is normally difficult to assure that all such updates are made, and when they are made, processing time is required just for that purpose.

While logical relations reduce redundancy by eliminating the need for redundant storage of information under other parents, they create a form of redundancy when physically paired logical children are used. Although IMS controls and assures the integrity of data in the two sets of paired logical children, the processing time for updating two segments rather than just one can become significant.

Data integrity is one of the fundamental concerns of the data-base world, and minimizing redundant data in update situations is one of the major steps in controlling integrity. In read-only situations, redundant data can be used to yield performance advantages without imperiling integrity.

Accessing Implications

Accessing across a logical relation from a physical or logical parent to a destination parent can be considerably slower than accessing from a physical parent to a physical child. If these physical children are contained in the same block as their physical parents, additional physical I/Os are avoided. But with logical relations, at least one block boundary must always be crossed, for the logical parents are always in different blocks from their logical children.

With unidirectional logical relations and with bidirectional logical relations with physical pairing, access is always made from a physical parent to a physical child to get the pointer to the associated destination (logical) parent. The destination parents are in separate blocks from their logical children, and thus an additional physical I/O is required to reach them after obtaining their pointers from their logical children.

With logical relations using virtual pairing, the situation can be more complex, depending on the direction of traversal. When going from a physical parent to a physical child (for pointers) and then on to a destination (logical) parent, the situation is the same as described above. But when traversing in the opposite direction—from a logical parent to a logical child and on to its destination (physical) parent— two additional factors become involved. First, every segment in the logical twin chain is in a separate block. Searching a long logical twin chain to find a pointer to a desired destination parent can become very expensive. Second, because the intersection segment contains only the concatenated key of its logical parent, the concatenated key of the destination (physical) parent must be materialized for presentation to the application program. This is necessary in order that the application program can have access to the concatenated key of the paired physical logical child that would have been present if physical pairing had been used. To materialize this concatenated key, DL/I must access each segment in the path from the destination parent up to its root.

Accessing across logical boundaries is to be avoided whenever possible. However, when a logical child is accessed via its physical parent, its logical (destination) parent is also accessed under the following conditions:

1. When retrieving or replacing a concatenated segment with data sensitivity to the logical parent.
2. When inserting a logical child (a counter in the logical parent must be incremented).
3. When deleting a logical child (a counter in the logical parent must be decremented).

Updating Implications

The frequency and type of updates is another major consideration of logical relations. Separate consideration must be given to updates of the logical parents and to updates of the logical children. Since logical relations eliminate redundancy that otherwise would exist if the logical parent segment types had to be replicated under other parents, it follows that updates to logical parent information need be done only once instead of several times. In this sense, the update implications of logical relations imply a savings of time.

The updating of logical children, on the other hand, can be more costly if the logical relation is bidirectional, because there may be two sets of logical child segments to be updated. With physical pairing, which employs two corresponding sets of logical children, any update to a segment in one set requires a similar update to a corresponding (paired) segment in the other set. With virtual pairing only one logical child segment is affected when updating a field, and only one segment is inserted or deleted although pointers in other segments will have to be adjusted.

In an information retrieval type of data base with little or no updating activity, performance is frequently better when logical relations are not used. By duplicating desired information so that it can be retrieved as part of (or at least as a physical child of) a segment already accessed, the desired information can be obtained more quickly than by accessing across a logical relation. But in an updating environment, the integrity benefit of not having duplicate information is usually considered to be well worth the performance impact of logical relations.

Reorganization Implications

Data-base reorganization presents another performance implication of logical relations, and the implication is more severe when using direct pointers. When direct pointers are involved, the reorganization of a data base means that other data bases which are logically related to it may also have to participate in the reorganization. This is because as segments are physically moved in the reorganization process, other data bases having direct pointers to those segments will need to have these pointers modified with new physical addresses. But with symbolic pointers which consist of the concatenated keys of the "target" segments, the physical movement of segments in a data-base reorganization does not require an alteration of their concatenated keys.

AN ALTERNATIVE TO LOGICAL RELATIONS

There is an alternative to logical relations that avoids the redundant duplication of segments. The "would-be" physical parent segments are given additional data fields containing the keys of the "would-be" logical parents. After accessing the "physical parent," the application program uses these key fields for accessing the desired "logical parents." This gives the same effect as logical relations, but all maintenance and use of pointers must be done by the application program rather than automatically by IMS. The characteristics of this approach are similar to those of symbolic pointers. Accessing logical parents by key values is frequently slower than when using direct pointers. But key-type pointers need not be changed when reorganizations occur. Further, physical child segments can be used to simulate logical child segments when intersection data is required.

This alternative approach is sometimes favored over logical relations because it avoids the complexities of defining and generating the logical data bases, and it minimizes the impact of reorganizations. It generally yields better performance by avoiding the interrogation of an intersection segment to find a destination parent. But on the other hand, pointer maintenance and a large part of the integrity concern are transferred from IMS to the application program. As the data-base structures and relationships become more complex, the appeal of this alternative approach quickly diminishes.

LOGICAL RELATION PERFORMANCE SUMMARY AND DESIGN GUIDELINES

This section summarizes the main guidelines presented in this chapter.

- Use unidirectional logical relations to traverse a logical boundary in both directions when the relationship in one direction is different (asynchronous) from the relationship in the reverse direction.
- Use bidirectional logical relations to traverse a logical boundary in both directions when the same type of relationship holds in both directions.
- Physical pairing gives faster accessing performance in one direction.
- Virtual pairing gives better space utilization, and it is expected to give better update performance by avoiding the double updates of logical children. But the savings in updates must be weighed against the additional pointer maintenance required.
- Try to avoid searching long logical twin chains with virtual pairing. They are a major adversary of good performance.
- Try to avoid logical twin chains ordered by key sequence. It is faster to insert first or last on the twin chain.
- In virtual pairing place the pointer (intersection) segment so that it is the physical child of the parent that defines the most heavily used path to the pointer segment, and as a logical child of the parent that defines the least heavily used path to it.
- The choice of symbolic or direct pointers exists in HDAM and HIDAM data bases and in logical child segments in a HISAM data base for pointing to segments in HD data bases. Symbolic pointers are always used to point into HISAM data bases. Direct pointers usually provide more rapid accessing, while symbolic pointers usually permit simpler and less time consuming reorganizations of the target data base.

10
SECONDARY INDEXES

INTRODUCTION

The wise use of secondary indexes is one of the more difficult and elusive aspects of data-base performance. Although secondary indexes can offer significant performance advantages when properly used, they can also pose some significant performance problems. Principles and guidelines for their proper use can be offered, but quantitative objective criteria are difficult to obtain.

DESCRIPTION

Secondary indexes are primarily a means of accessing the occurrences of a data-base segment in some order other than their normal key sequence order. The concept of secondary indexes is illustrated in Figure 10-1. The secondary index is a HISAM-like root-only data base separate from the main data base being accessed. The format and content of the index root segments is depicted in Figure 10-2.

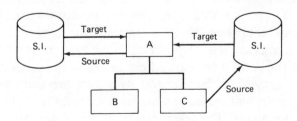

Figure 10-1. The concept of secondary indexes.

NON-UNIQUE PTR.	DELETE BYTE	DIRECT POINTER	KEY FIELD			DATA FIELD	CONCAT. KEY	USER DATA
			SHARED INDEX	SEARCH FIELD	SUBSEQUENCE FIELD			

Non-Unique Pointer – Four byte pointer to next Index Pointer Segment in the VSAM key is non-unique.

Delete Byte – One byte.

Direct Pointer – Four byte pointer to the Target Segment (for HDAM or HIDAM)

Shared Index – One byte constant for multiple indexes.

Search Field – The search field for which a Target Segment is to be accessed. (One to five fields from the Source Segment.)

Subsequence Field – Used to provide uniqueness to non-unique search fields. (Zero to five fields from the Source Segment.)

Data Field – Zero to five data fields from the Source Segment. (System maintained.)

Concatenated Key – Concatenated key of Target Segment. (Present only if symbolic pointers are specified.)

User Data – A field available to an application program when processing the index as a separate data base. (Not system maintained.)

Figure 10–2. Index pointer segment.

The fields of primary interest are discussed in the body of this chapter.

Secondary indexes are constructed and maintained by IMS. The segment to be accessed in the main data base is called the *target* segment, and it is located by means of either the direct pointer or the concatenated key. The target segment can be any segment in the data base. If it is other than the root segment, the application program processes a logical view of the main data base in which the target segment is the root. The search field provides the criteria by which the target segment is chosen, and its values are extracted from a *source* segment, which can be the target segment itself or any of its dependent segments. The segments of the index data base are called *index pointer* segments.

GENERAL PERFORMANCE CONCEPTS

Retrieval Implications

The advantage of using a secondary index comes when doing a series of retrievals for segments from a small percentage of data-base records according to some common criteria other than their normal key. Otherwise, using secondary indexes can be costly. Since the index itself is a separate HISAM-like data base, an indexed access to a target segment requires one or more physical I/Os into the index in addition to the I/O for the target segment. In addition, because the target segments are accessed in some order other than their key sequence, they are accessed randomly. This can mean more physical I/Os and more access arm movement than would otherwise be required.

While the added cost of accessing via a secondary index for a small number of records can be considerably less than the alternative cost of searching the entire data base for the desired segments, this advantage tends to disappear quickly as the number of indexed accesses grows. This is illustrated by considering the extreme case of retrieving a segment from every data-base record. On the one hand, a sequential scan of every data-base record followed by a possible sort can be done. But if using a secondary index, a random access to the target segment in each record plus the additional I/Os for accessing the index for each record is required. Without the sort, the former method is clearly faster. With large data bases, experience shows that even with the sort, the sequential scan can be significantly faster than the indexed random accessing. Identifying the break-even point is very difficult to do analytically. It is usually done by modeling or simulation of some type (Chapter 18 discusses modeling). Many practitioners state that no more than 10 to 20 percent of the database records should be accessed via a secondary index.

Update Implications

The implications of data-base updates on secondary index performance can be even more striking than that of retrievals. If source or target segments are inserted or deleted, corresponding entries must be added to or deleted from the index. Because the index is a HISAM-

like data base (which performs well for retrieval when well organized, but not so well for updates), the update of the index can be
more costly than the update to the data base itself. Furthermore,
after a number of updates the index itself frequently needs to be
reorganized to avoid its own excessive performance degradation.

Updating the source field in an existing segment is even more
costly. An entry must be deleted from the index, and a new entry
must be added. Thus two updates to the index are required. The
potential performance advantage of retrievals can quickly be lost in
a data base that is subject to frequent updates.

One other point must be made. There are times when several secondary indexes will be used for efficient accessing of a data base
from different perspectives. If all these indexes must be updated each
time there is a data-base update, the performance implications of
updates become proportionally more severe.

SPECIAL INDEXING CHARACTERISTICS

Unique/Non-Unique Keys

Index pointer segments for unique source field values are stored in
a VSAM Key Sequenced Data Set (KSDS). This corresponds with a
HISAM primary data set. In this discussion, we will refer to these
source field values as keys. Whenever non-unique keys are present,
two data sets are used. Pointer segments for any unique key values,
and for the first occurrence of all non-unique values, are placed in
the VSAM KSDS. Pointer segments for all duplicate key values are
stored into a VSAM Entry Sequenced Data Set (ESDS). This corresponds with a HISAM overflow data set. The ESDS pointer segments are chained to their KSDS counterparts in a last-in-first-out
(LIFO) manner.

Duplicate keys pose performance implications. An additional I/O
is required when going from the KSDS to the ESDS. In addition,
the ESDS tends to become poorly organized rather quickly when updates are performed. Pointer segments for duplicate key values are
likely to be in different blocks, thus necessitating additional I/Os
when searching them. Index reorganizations are required more frequently.

A concept called *subsequence fields* can be used to avoid these
disadvantages of non-unique keys. A subsequence field is an addi-

tional field in the pointer segment that is concatenated onto the key field in order to produce uniqueness. There can be up to five subsequence fields concatenated together in a pointer segment. Subsequence fields may be constructed from values of other fields in the source segments, or if necessary they may be constructed from the source segment's Relative Byte Address (RBA) or from its concatenated key values. Because unique combinations are obtained by appending subsequence fields onto non-unique keys, the index pointer segments are all stored in the KSDS, and the separate ESDS and its disadvantages are avoided. Application program accessing specifies only the key, and not also the subsequence field, but the corresponding target segments for that key are obtained in the order specified by the subsequence fields.

Direct and Symbolic Pointers

Index pointer segments point to their target segments by means of direct pointers or by symbolic pointers. Direct pointers are four-byte RBA addresses of the target segments. Symbolic pointers are the concatenated keys of the target segments. These are the same types of pointers that have been described for logical relations, and their relative advantages and disadvantages are the same as in logical relations. HISAM target segments require symbolic pointers. Target segments in HDAM or HIDAM data bases can be accessed by either direct or symbolic pointers. With direct pointers, access is made directly to the target segment with one I/O. With symbolic pointers, DL/I must search for the target segment, and several I/Os could be required. On the other hand, a secondary index using symbolic pointers does not have to be reorganized when its target data base is reorganized, whereas an index using direct pointers must participate in the reorganization.

Full and Sparse Indexing

A *full index* contains entries for all values in the source fields. On the other hand, a *sparse index* contains entries only for selected values. To illustrate, consider a lending institution that deals with loans of various types such as VA, FHA, and Conventional. Suppose further that a secondary index is to be used to locate just the VA loans. This is an example of a sparse index.

The primary advantage of a sparse index is speed. Because the index contains entries for only the desired source field values, DL/I does not have to search through preliminary entries to find the entries for the desired target segments. Thus the index search is faster than with a full index.

Another, but more remote, possible advantage of sparse indexes is the possibility of indexing only the source field values that are subject to few if any updates, while using conventional accessing for the other source field values. Also, there is the possibility, through programming, of bringing an entire short sparse index into main memory and then searching it without further index I/Os.

Including Data in the Index Segments

Since the secondary index is a root only HISAM-like data base, it can be processed independently of the data base it is supporting. To take advantage of this capability, up to five data fields from the source segment may be loaded into the index pointer segments when the index is constructed. The purpose of this feature is to permit rapid inquiry and simple updating by accessing a relatively short index as opposed to the index plus a relatively long target data base. Although DL/I poses some restrictions to preserve the integrity of the index, significant performance advantages are possible. Note that updating in this sense means updating only in the index and not in the main data base.

SECONDARY INDEXING VS. LOGICAL RELATIONS

Secondary indexes and logical relations have some common characteristics. Both can be used to restructure a data base, and both can be used to access segments in some order other than the segment's key. To illustrate, consider the data base shown in Figure 10-3.

Straightforward processing can examine the skills possessed by a given person. But a requirement to examine the people having a given skill requires a restructuring of the data base. With logical relations the two data bases can be combined and restructured to present the logical view of Figure 10-4.

With a secondary index, as shown in Figure 10-5, the single NAME data base can be restructured into the view shown in Figure 10-6.

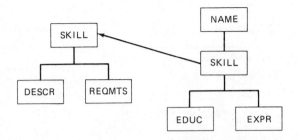

Figure 10-3. Logically related SKILL and NAME data bases.

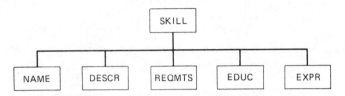

Figure 10-4. Logical data base starting with SKILL.

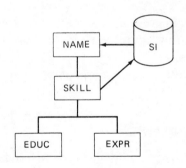

Figure 10-5. NAME data base with a secondary index.

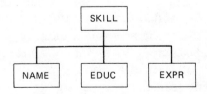

Figure 10-6. Logical data base from secondary indexing.

Situation	Use Logical Relation	Use Secondary Index
1. Single Physical Data Base	*	*
2. Multiple Physical Data Bases	*	
3. Enter at Root Segment	*	*
4. Enter at Dependent Segment		*
5. Provide Recursive (Bill of Material) Relationship	*	
6. Provide Paths Between Segments Related by M-M Mapping	*	
7. Provide upward Path Between Segments Related by 1-M (Parent-Child) Mapping	*	*

Figure 10–7. Relative uses of secondary indexes vs. logical relations.

The fundamental difference between secondary indexes and logical relations should now be apparent. Secondary indexes deal with a single physical data base, whereas logical relations can deal with, and combine segments from, several physical data bases. Further, secondary indexes can be used to make initial entry into the data base at some level other than the root, but logical relations are not used for initial entry.

Figure 10–7 presents further selection criteria.

PERFORMANCE GUIDELINES

In summary, the following guidelines are offered for the use of secondary indexes:

1. Secondary indexes are good for retrieving segments from a small percentage of data-base records. They are used primarily for random inquiry via a secondary key.
2. Secondary indexes are also useful for entering a data base at some segment other than its root.
3. When retrieving segments from a large percentage of data-base records, a sequential scan of the data base, possibly followed

by a sort, is usually faster than retrieving segments in the desired order via a secondary index.

4. In a large data base subject to frequent updates that would require index modification, secondary indexes should be avoided, if at all possible. Consider scanning and sorting, or logical relations.

11
POINTER OPTIONS

INTRODUCTION

While there are many types of pointers used in DL/I data bases, in this chapter we will discuss the pointers used by DL/I for locating a particular segment in a HDAM or HIDAM data base. These are the pointers that are located in a segment's prefix (Figure 11-1) and which are specified in the Data Base Descriptor block (DBD). Many choices and combinations of these pointers are available. Because of the many "pointer options" available and the varying effects they have on the performance of the data base, a good understanding of pointer options and their implications is essential for designing a data base for good performance.

Before discussing the various pointer options, it will be well at this point to remind ourselves of certain accessing characteristics of the four major DL/I access methods.

In HSAM and HISAM segments are accessed in hierarchical sequence. This sequence is established by the physical adjacency of the segments. In HISAM special pointers (not of the type we will be considering in this chapter) assist in establishing hierarchical sequence to and from segments stored in the overflow data set. The prefix pointers, which are the primary subject of this chapter, are not available for HSAM and HISAM data bases.

In HDAM and HIDAM, segments are loaded in hierarchical sequence, but they are not necessarily placed physically according to their hierarchical sequence. They may be (and sometimes are) processed in hierarchical sequence, but the majority of the time they are processed in a random, nonhierarchical manner in which DL/I goes directly from a parent to the first occurrence of any of its child segment types without having to pass through intermediate segments.

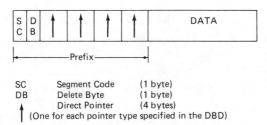

SC   Segment Code   (1 byte)
DB   Delete Byte   (1 byte)
       Direct Pointer   (4 bytes)
↑ (One for each pointer type specified in the DBD)

Figure 11-1. Direct pointers in segment prefix.

In both cases the appropriate pointer is used to locate the next segment to be accessed.

TYPES OF POINTERS

The pointers DL/I uses to locate segments in HD organizations can be categorized according to their usage and to their implementation. With regard to usage, these pointers can be grouped into two major categories: (1) those used for hierarchical accessing and (2) those used for random accessing. This latter category can be further subdivided into random accessing in physical relationships and random accessing in logical relationships. Each of these categories and their pointers will be discussed in the sections to follow.

To be complete, pointer classification according to implementation must also be mentioned. Here we have direct pointers and symbolic pointers. *Direct* pointers, which are the four-byte addresses in the prefix, give the physical displacement of the target segment from the beginning of its data set. It is direct pointers that we have discussed thus far and that we will be discussing throughout most of this chapter. The other type of pointers, *symbolic* pointers, will be treated in a special section later in the chapter.

The remaining sections of the chapter describe each of the pointer types according to their usage, and discuss the implementation options.

Pointers for Hierarchical Accessing

There are two types of pointers in this category, Hierarchical Forward Pointers (HF) and Hierarchical Backward Pointers (HB). These pointers are used in HD organizations for processing segments within a data-base record in their hierarchical sequence. This is a rare way of processing HDAM and HIDAM data bases, but it is appropriate when sequential processing within a data-base record is required. If processing is to proceed more directly from a parent to one of its child segment types chosen at random, hierarchical pointers should not be specified.

Hierarchical Forward (HF).   Hierarchical Forward pointers (Figure 11–2) are to be specified when processing is to proceed in a hierarchical sequence, segment by segment, from a root to some "last" segment within the data-base record. This type of pointer is usually advantageous if all segments in a data-base record are to be processed in order, and it may also be advantageous for skip-sequential processing.

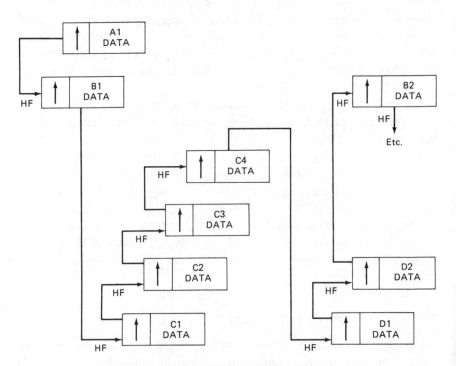

Figure 11–2. Hierarchical Forward pointers.

Hierarchical Backward (HB).   If hierarchical pointers are used and if the data-base records are subject to frequent deletions of segments, Hierarchical Backward pointers (Figure 11–3) should be considered in addition to the Hierarchical Forward pointers. When a segment is deleted, Hierarchical Backward pointers are used by DL/I to quickly relocate the predecessor segment so that the pointer in the predecessor may be changed to point to the segment just beyond the one being deleted. Otherwise, DL/I reverts back to the parent segment and works its way forward again to find the predecessor segment. Hierarchical Backward pointers should be used only when doing many deletes in large data-base records. Their disadvantage is that they must be updated whenever segments are inserted or deleted. They are used by DL/I solely as an efficiency device for deletion operations, and not for any type of accessing.

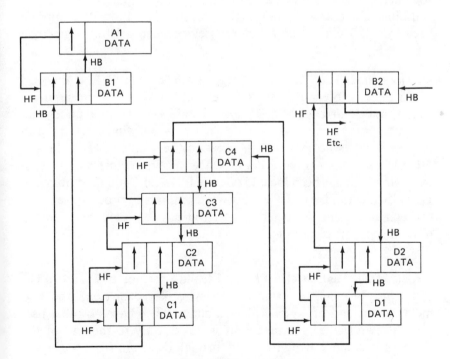

Figure 11–3. Hierarchical Backward pointers.

Random Access Pointers for Physical Relations

These are the pointers used by HDAM and HIDAM for accessing from a parent to a physical child and from a segment to its physical twin. All random accessing within physical relationships is done using these pointers. The four types of pointers in this category are the following:

- Physical Child First (PCF).
- Physical Twin Forward (PTF).
- Physical Child Last (PCL).
- Physical Twin Backward (PTB).

The Physical Child First and Physical Twin Forward pointers are used together for most accessing activities, and they will be described together. Physical Child Last pointers are used separately for a special kind of accessing. The fourth type, Physical Twin Backward, is used by DL/I only as an efficiency device when deleting segments.

Physical Child First (PCF) and Physical Twin Forward (PTF). Physical Child First pointers are used by DL/I to go directly from a parent to the first occurrence of any physical child segment type under that parent. These pointers, along with the Physical Twin Forward pointers, are DL/I's normal way of accessing segments in HIDAM and HDAM data bases (Figure 11-4). Once the first segment of a physical twin chain has been located (via the Physical Child First pointer), DL/I then uses Physical Twin Forward pointers to proceed, segment by segment, from the beginning of the physical twin chain to the desired segment occurrence.

Physical Child Last (PCL). Physical Child Last pointers (Figure 11-5) are useful when inserting or retrieving keyed or nonkeyed segments at the end of a physical twin chain. They have no other use. They provide DL/I the means of going directly to the end of the chain rather than having to ripple through the chain from beginning to end. For accesses to the end of long physical twin chains, the re-

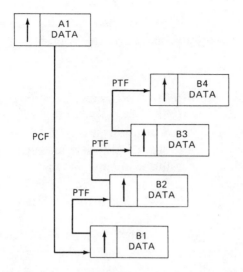

Figure 11–4. Physical Twin Forward pointers.

sulting savings can more than offset the additional overhead of modifying this pointer when a segment is inserted at or deleted from the end of the chain. The Physical Child Last pointer provides access only to the last segment on a physical twin chain. DL/I does not

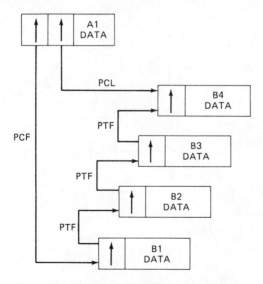

Figure 11–5. Physical Child Last pointer.

move backward to access prior twins of the last segment. Physical Child Last pointers require that Physical Child First pointers also be present.

Physical Twin Backward (PTB). Physical Twin Backward pointers (Figure 11–6), like Hierarchical Backward pointers, should be used only when large numbers of deletions are expected on long physical twin chains. They permit more efficient deletion operations, and they play no other role in accessing segments. When a segment is deleted, the Physical Twin Forward pointer in the preceeding twin must be altered to point to the twin that immediately follows the deleted segment. After locating the segment to be deleted, if there are no Physical Twin Backward pointers, DL/I returns to the parent segment, and then relocates the twin chain, and works its way forward to relocate the segment just prior to the deleted segment. But when backward pointers are present, DL/I can find the predecessor segment immediately by referring to the backward pointer in the segment being deleted. The disadvantages of Physical Twin Backward point-

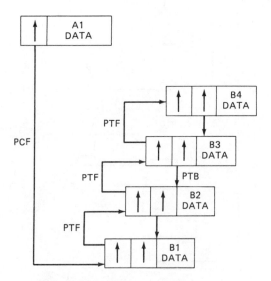

Figure 11–6. Physical Twin Backward pointers.

ers is that they take up space in a segment's prefix and that they must be maintained when insertions and deletions are made to the twin chain in which they are used.

Random Access Pointers for Logical Relations

HDAM and HIDAM use the following six pointer types for traversing logical relations:

- Logical Parent (LP).
- Logical Child First (LCF).
- Logical Twin Forward (LTF).
- Physical Parent (PP).
- Logical Child Last (LCL).
- Logical Twin Backward (LTB).

The first of these pointers, Logical Parent, is used in all logical relations to go from a logical child to its logical parent. The Logical Child First, Logical Twin Forward, and Physical Parent pointers work together in bidirectional virtual logical relations, and they will be discussed together. The Logical Child Last pointer is used separately for special accessing to the end of the logical twin chain. The last of these pointer types, Logical Twin Backward, serves DL/I as an efficiency device when performing deletions in logical twin chains.

Logical Parent (LP). Logical Parent pointers are used in the implementation of all varieties of logical relations. As shown in Figure 11-7, Logical Parent pointers reside in the prefixes of logical child segments, and they point to the associated logical parent segments. Thus Logical Parent pointers provide the final link in going from a physical parent to a logical parent. Starting with the physical parent, DL/I proceeds via the Physical Child First pointer to the beginning of the twin chain which serves both as physical children of the physical parent and as logical children of the associated logical parents. DL/I then uses the Physical Twin Forward pointers to proceed to the desired segment occurrence in this chain. It then uses the Logical Parent pointer to access the associated logical parent. The combined data portion contents of the logical child and its logical parent can

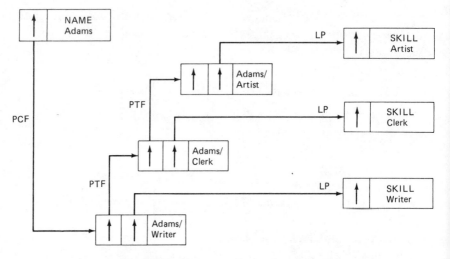

Figure 11–7. Logical Parent pointers.

be returned to the application program as though the combination were all a child of the physical parent.

Logical Child First (LCF), Logical Twin Forward (LTF), and Physical Parent (PP). These three pointer types (Figure 11-8) are used in implementing virtually paired bidirectional logical relations. They provide the means of traversing from a logical parent to its associated physical parents. The Logical Child First pointer provides the path from the logical parent to the first segment of the logical twin chain, and the Logical Twin Forward pointers provide the paths from each logical twin occurrence to the next logical twin occurrence. DL/I then uses the Physical Parent pointer to go from a selected logical twin occurrence to its physical parent. The combined data portion contents of the logical child and its physical parent can be returned to the application program as though this combination were all a child of the logical parent.

Logical Child Last (LCL). The Logical Child Last pointer (Figure 11-9) plays a role similar to the Physical Child Last pointer. It provides immediate access to the last segment of a long logical twin chain by enabling DL/I to go directly from a logical parent to the last segment

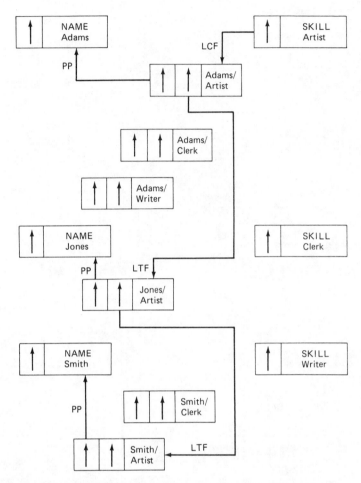

Figure 11–8. Logical Child First pointer, Logical Twin Forward pointers, and Physical Parent pointers.

occurrence in the chosen logical twin chain. Using the Physical Parent pointer, DL/I can then access the physical parent of that last logical twin. But these are the only segments that can be accessed via the Logical Child Last pointer. DL/I does not move backward in the logical twin chain to access any prior logical twin segment. A Logical Child Last pointer can be implemented only if the Logical Child First pointer is also specified.

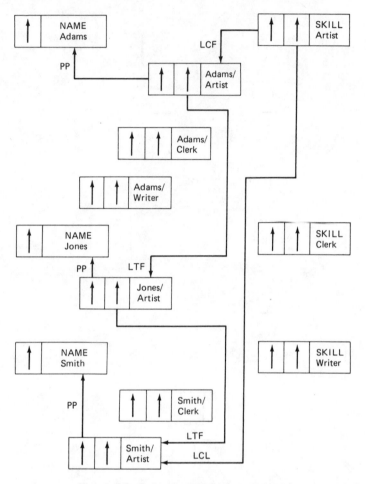

Figure 11-9. Logical Child Last pointer.

Logical Twin Backward (LTB). Logical Twin Backward pointers (Figure 11-10) may be specified for logical twin chains in virtually paired bidirectional logical relations. Their only purpose is to improve deletion performance, and when used they provide the same service for logical twin deletions that Physical Twin Backward pointers provide for physical twin deletions. Logical Twin Backward pointers require that Logical Twin Forward pointers also be specified.

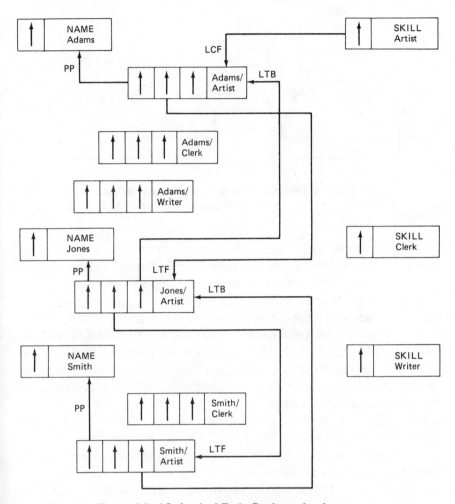

Figure 11-10. Logical Twin Backward pointers.

DIRECT VS. SYMBOLIC POINTERS

As illustrated in Figure 11-11, there are two fundamental implementation categories of pointers: direct and symbolic.

Direct pointers are normally used for all physical and logical relationships in HDAM or HIDAM data bases. Symbolic pointers can
also be used within the HD organizations. Logical child segments in a
HISAM data base that point to logical parents in the HD data orga-

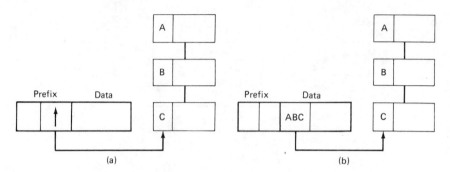

Figure 11–11a. Direct pointer (a four-byte physical address).
Figure 11–11b. Symbolic pointer (a concatenated key).

nizations may also use either symbolic or direct pointers. On the other hand, all logical children in any data base that point to logical parents in a HISAM data base must use symbolic pointers.

Direct pointers are contained in the prefix of a segment, and they contain four-byte physical addresses of the segments being referenced. Thus the segment being referenced can be accessed with at most one physical I/O. Symbolic pointers, on the other hand, reside within the segment's data portion, and they consist of the concatenated keys of the segments in a path leading to the referenced segment from its root. Using that portion of the concatenated key that pertains to the root segment, DL/I locates the root, either by randomizing or by referring to an index. Using the remainder of the concatenated key as qualifiers, the desired segment is located in the normal manner by sequentially scanning the dependent segments (HISAM) or by following the appropriate direct pointers (HDAM or HIDAM). Depending on the distance of the referenced segment from its root, several physical I/Os could be required.

The fundamental advantage of direct pointers is fast access (no more than one physical I/O) to a desired segment. Their disadvantage is that whenever a data base is reorganized and its segments are physically relocated, all other data bases that use direct pointers (in logical relations) to point to segments in the reorganized data base must have these pointers updated with the new segment locations. Thus these other data bases must also participate in the reorganization process.

Symbolic pointers, on the other hand, avoid the reorganization problem since the concatenated keys do not change when their target segments are physically moved. But they may require several physical I/Os to access desired segments via their concatenated keys because DL/I must search for these segments.

SUMMARY OF POINTER OPTIONS

Figure 11–12 summarizes the various types of pointers and gives the fundamental use of each type.

POINTER TYPE		USED FOR	PREREQUISITE
Hierarchical Forward	HF	Hierarchical Accessing	
Hierarchical Backward	HB	Delete Efficiency (Hierarchical Chain)	HF
Physical Child First	PCF	Random Physical Accessing (Parent to First Twin)	
Physical Twin Forward	PTF	Random Physical Accessing (Twin to Next Twin)	
Physical Child Last	PCL	Random Physical Accessing (Last Twin Segment Only)	PCF
Physical Twin Backward	PTB	Delete Efficiency (Physical Twin Chain)	PTF
Logical Parent	LP	Random Logical Accessing (Logical Child to Logical Parent)	
Logical Child First	LCF	Random Logical Accessing (Logical Parent to First Logical Twin)	
Logical Twin Forward	LTF	Random Logical Accessing (Logical Twin to Next Logical Twin)	
Physical Parent	PP	Random Logical Accessing (Logical Child to Physical Parent)	
Logical Child Last	LCL	Random Logical Accessing (Logical Parent to Last Logical Twin Only)	LCF
Logical Twin Backward	LTB	Delete Efficiency (Logical Twin Chain)	LTF

Figure 11–12. Pointer option summary.

POINTER OPTION GUIDELINES

The following guidelines are offered as performance implications to consider when selecting the pointer options to be used:

1. Physical/Logical Child First and Physical/Logical Twin Forward pointers are the standard means of accessing in physical/logical relations.
2. Use Hierarchical pointers only when accessing segments in hierarchical sequence.
3. Physical/Logical Twin Last pointers provide the fastest way of accessing the last segment on a physical/logical twin chain.
4. Use Physical/Logical Twin Backward pointers in dependent segments only when doing frequent deletions from long physical/logical twin chains.
5. Use Physical Twin Forward and Backward pointers in HIDAM root segments if sequential processing of the roots is required. This avoids references back to the index for each root.
6. Direct pointers generally provide faster accessing than symbolic pointers.
7. Symbolic pointers generally mean faster reorganizations.

12
PHYSICAL DESIGN GUIDELINES

GENERAL

To conclude this treatment of the performance aspects of DL/I data bases, a number of practical design guidelines will be presented. These guidelines are intended to enhance DL/I data-base efficiency with respect to performance and space utilization, and they are gathered from several sources (including the author's own experience).

Although they are by no means all-inclusive, the guidelines presented here represent necessary design considerations when making and evaluating physical design choices and in refining the logical design. Guidelines for data bases, segments, physical twin chains, pointer options, logical relations, and secondary indexes will be presented in turn.

DATA BASES

Avoid Long Data-Base Records.   Data-base records that fit within a block are ideal in terms of processing time (only one physical I/O for all the segments) although they may waste storage space. If some of the data-base records are significantly longer than the others because of a large variation of the number of occurrences of certain segment types, consider separating those segments into secondary data set groups.

Do Not Create Many Data Bases.   Separate physical data bases usually imply logical relations. They may also imply more frequent and more complex reorganization. All of these factors can adversely affect performance. To the extent permitted by security, integrity, and other performance considerations, the number of separate physical data bases should be as small as possible.

Split Large Data Bases.   On the other hand, there are several reasons for splitting large data bases. For example, if most entries are made through a segment other than the root, performance can frequently be improved by making that segment a root of a separate, logically related data base. Separate data bases are a way of reducing redundancy. Also, a judicious splitting could mean smaller data bases to reorganize.

Reduce Contention from Program Isolation.   With program isolation, the entire data-base record is made unavailable to other programs until the program moves to another record. Updated segments remain unavailable until a sync point occurs. This can be desirable from the standpoints of security and integrity, but it can also pose severe performance implications on contending programs.

One alternative is to shorten the data-base record by placing some of its segments into another record, which would then be available to the contending programs. Another possibility is to build tables in main memory with information extracted from the data-base record. Also, the enqueing program should move to the next record as quickly as possible.

Use Compaction.   Compaction is an excellent way of reducing the space requirements of data stored in the data base. This can lead to more segments per block, which implies a performance improvement as well as a space saving. The cost is that space and time are required for the compaction and decompaction routines to reside and to function, but this is usually a minimal consideration.

SEGMENTS

Frequently Accessed Segments Should Be Kept As Close to the Root As Possible.   The closer a segment is to its root, the greater the likelihood of its being in the same block as its root. When a root is accessed, all the other segments in its block are thus available in the buffer pool without additional physical I/Os. In addition, with HISAM, even if a segment is not in the same block as its root, the closer it is to the root, the fewer intervening segments that have to be scanned to find it. Fewer intervening blocks mean fewer physical I/Os.

Fewer Segment Types Generally Mean Less Reorganization Time. Fewer segment types mean fewer pointers to be resolved during reorganization.

Consider Segment Prefix Size.   If the segment prefix is larger than the data portion, consider combining the segment with its parent. This can reduce the space required for segment overhead, and it can improve performance by having fewer segments (and one less segment level) to access and also by having more segment information in a block. But there can be disadvantages, as suggested in the next section.

Be Cautious about Combining Segments.   Injudicious combining of segments can have an adverse effect on security and integrity. By combining unrelated fields (even though attributes of the same entity), programs may access segments containing information not belonging to them, and update integrity becomes much more difficult to control. Also, combining segments may mean creating redundant occurrences of the same data.

Consider Separating Segments of Varying Sizes.   One of the primary purposes of data set groups is to separate segments of varying sizes into groups such that the segments in each group are of similar size. This is an excellent way of conserving space. In many situations it can also improve performance, although in other situations it might have adverse performance implications.

Consider Variable-Length Segments if a Segment Has One Occurrence of a Child Segment Type That May or May Not Exist.   By making the parent variable-length and including the fields of the child when they exist, storage space can be saved and all of the information can be accessed with one DL/I call. But this can be counterproductive if other applications access the parent only.

Be Cautious about Updates to Variable-Length Segments.   Updates that change the length of a segment can have a significant performance impact if the updated segment no longer fits into the storage space from which it was retrieved.

PHYSICAL TWIN CHAINS

Break up Long Twin Chains.   Searching long twin chains can be one of the most serious obstacles to good performance. Twin chains can be broken into sections according to generic key groupings, and each section can be accessed through an intermediate physical parent or through secondary indexing. Other techniques for breaking up long twin chains are also available.

Consider Nonkeyed Segments to Reduce Overhead of Inserts and Deletes.   Nonkeyed segments are inserted or deleted at the beginning or the end of a twin chain, or at the current position within the chain. Time is not expended searching for the right position within the chain.

POINTER OPTIONS

Physical Child and Physical Twin Pointers Are Most Frequently Used. These are the standard pointers used by HDAM and HIDAM. Other pointer types should be used only if specifically needed for function or performance.

Use Backward Pointers Only for Long Twin Chains Subject to Frequent Deletions.   Backward pointers save time in deletion operations, but they must be updated when inserting new segments. They are very effective for large-volume updates on long twin chains. But the prefix space and the maintenance they require may offset their benefit in cases of low deletion activity or when the twin chain is relatively short.

Direct Pointers Generally Imply Fewer Physical I/Os.   A direct pointer contains the physical address of the block containing the segment to be accessed, and at most one physical I/O is required to retrieve that block. A symbolic pointer, on the other hand, contains the concatenated keys of the segments encountered in the direct physical path from a root to the segment to be accessed. In this case, DL/I finds the required segment using the qualifications indicated by the concatenated keys to search from the segment's root according to the rules of the DL/I access method being used. If the required segment is not in the same block as its root, DL/I will perform a physical I/O for each block encountered in the search process, unless such blocks are already in the buffer pools.

Symbolic Pointers Generally Permit Independent Data-Base Reorganization.   Because symbolic pointers do not change when the physical location of segments change, logically related data bases can be reorganized one at a time when they are connected by symbolic pointers.

LOGICAL RELATIONS

For Bidirectional Virtual Pairing, Place the Real Logical Child Under the Parent in the Most Frequently Used Path to the Child.   The path between physical parent and child can usually be traversed more rapidly than the path between logical parent and child. The more frequently used path should be the one offering the performance advantage.

Bidirectional Physical Pairing Provides Sequential Ordering of the Destination Parent.   With bidirectional virtual pairing, when the destination parent is the logical parent, sequential ordering is not available. With physical pairing, sequential ordering of the destination parent is provided in both directions.

Searching Logical Twin Chains Can Be Costly.   In a large data base, it is rare for adjacent logical twins to be in the same block. Thus many physical I/Os may be required when searching them—that is, one I/O for each twin.

SECONDARY INDEXES

Secondary Indexes Are Most Suitable for Frequent Accesses to a Small Percentage of Data-Base Records.   If accessing a large percentage of data-base records, it is frequently faster to scan all of them sequentially and thus avoid the cost of accesses to the secondary index and the random accesses to the target segments. Not having a secondary index also means not having to update that index when updating the data base.

Avoid Indexing When Source or Target Segments Are Subject to Frequent Updates.   When source fields are updated and when source or target segments are inserted or deleted, corresponding updates to the secondary index are also made. The time required is compounded if several secondary indexes are involved.

Sparse Indexes May Reduce the Number of I/Os Needed to Find a Target.   I/Os can be reduced because sparse indexes are shorter than full indexes. And because sparse indexes contain only certain values, they may not need to be reorganized as often.

PART IV
PERFORMANCE ASPECTS OF
THE SYSTEM ENVIRONMENT

13
BUFFER POOLS AND THE STORY THEY TELL

FUNCTION AND DESCRIPTION

Buffer pools are areas of virtual storage set aside for holding blocks (or control intervals) read from or written to secondary storage. In this discussion we will loosely refer to secondary storage as disk storage.

It is desirable that the size of a buffer be as close as possible to the size of the block that will occupy it. The buffer must be at least as large as the block. Because blocks of various lengths can be encountered, buffers of different sizes are needed. This is accomplished by creating a buffer pool in virtual storage in such a way that the pool is subdivided into subpools. Each subpool contains a set of buffers of a given size, which can vary from subpool to subpool. The subpool buffer size and the number of buffers in each subpool are specified at system initialization time.

The buffer lengths provided by the subpools and the number of buffers available in each subpool are critical performance parameters. Too few buffers of the needed sizes mean additional physical I/Os in support of the DL/I calls. On the other hand, too many buffers mean wasted storage space and an increased paging rate. The optimum choice of size and number of buffers is very elusive. It requires a thorough analysis of the segment sizes and the expected frequencies of accessing and updating each segment type. Some guidelines will be presented at the end of this chapter.

In each subpool the buffers are chained according to their use. The most recently used buffer is at the top of the "use chain," and the least recently used is at the bottom. Whenever a buffer is referenced for an input or an output operation, it is placed at the top of the chain. Whenever a buffer is needed in an input operation to receive a block from disk, the least recently used (LRU) buffer is selected. The rationale is that the least recently used buffer is less likely to contain information still needed by the application program.

General Characteristics

There can be two buffer pools: one for data bases using VSAM and one for data bases using ISAM/OSAM. While their functions are similar, they are formatted differently, and the eligible buffer sizes are somewhat different. Although the sizes presented below have been quite stable over IMS and VSAM releases, the reader should keep in mind that they could become release-dependent in the future.

VSAM Buffer Sizes.   For VSAM data bases, eleven buffer sizes are available as follows:

512	16,384
1024	20,480
2048	24,576
4096	28,672
8192	32,768
12,288	

Note that the smallest buffer size is 512 bytes, and each eligible size is double the previous size up to 8192 bytes. After 8192 bytes, each eligible size is 4096 bytes larger than the previous size, up to 32,768 bytes.

We want to select buffer sizes that are as close as possible, but not less than, the block sizes to be encountered. For VSAM data clusters, valid CI sizes are as follows:

- Any multiple of 512 up to 8192 bytes.
- Any multiple of 2048 for CIs between 8192 bytes and 32,768 bytes.

For VSAM index clusters, valid CI sizes are 512, 1024, 2048, and 4096 bytes.

ISAM/OSAM Buffer Sizes.   For ISAM/OSAM data bases, the following buffer sizes are available:

>   512
>   1024
>   2048
> .
> .
> .

any multiple of 2048
> .
> .
> .

>   32,768

Again, we want to choose buffer sizes as close as possible to, but not less than, the block sizes to be encountered. Valid block sizes for ISAM/OSAM data bases can be any size between 18 and 32,768 bytes.

TYPES OF BUFFER ACTIVITY

There are several types of activities that can cause physical reads into or writes out of the buffers. These activities are described in the following sections.

Reading into Buffers

There are two reasons for reading blocks of information from the data base into the buffers. The primary reason is to satisfy (when necessary) an application program's read requests for segments. A second type of reading may occur as part of DL/I's search of the data base when trying to find the most desirable block to receive a segment being inserted. If a suitable block is not available in the buffers, one or more additional blocks will have to be read. Control Interval (CI) and Control Area (CA) splits may also be involved.

When a block is read from disk into a buffer, the buffer pool containing the smallest buffers that will hold the block is selected by the system. The least recently used buffer will receive the incoming block, and this buffer will be rechained to the top (most recently used position) of its use queue. If this LRU buffer contains altered data, a space write must occur to write the buffer to the data base so that it can then become available to receive the block being read.

It should be noted that if there are enough buffers, high-level index entries, which may be frequently accessed, tend to stay in the buffer pool.

Writing from Buffers

When an application program performs a data-base update operation by issuing a Replace, Insert, or Delete call, the only direct action IMS takes at that time is to update the contents of the buffers containing the affected segments. Physical writes to the disk are not made at these times. The time required for physical writes is conserved by deferring these writes as long as possible, and by grouping them so that whenever a physical write is necessary, many others can be done at the same time. This also eases the problem of backout if the program malfunctions before completion or checkpoint. Thus physical writes are performed as needed by the system and not as requested by the application program.

The ideal situation is that all updates are saved in the buffer pool until *synchronization point* (sync point) time. A sync point is a point of commitment which occurs at program termination or at a checkpoint call. At sync point time, all of the physical I/Os are performed at once. This is the action taken whenever possible. But occasions arise when buffers must be written before sync point time. This situation occurs when all buffers have been filled, and a physical write must be used to write out a buffer in order to free it for receiving a new block that the application program is trying to read. Thus the following types of writes can occur in support of these requirements: Sync Point Writes, Space Writes, and Background Writes. We will treat each in turn.

Sync Point Writes. Sync Point Writes occur when a data base is closed (normally at program termination) or when a program terminates abnormally (ABEND). They also occur as the result of checkpoint (CHKP) calls within the application program. All buffers that have been changed since the last sync point (or program initiation) are written to the data base.

Whenever a buffer receives an update, IMS instructs VSAM to set a flag for that buffer and to assign an alteration ID. The same alteration ID is used for all updates by a program between sync points. When a program reaches a new sync point, all marked buffers containing the alteration ID for the completed sync point interval are written to disk.

Space Writes.   A Space Write is the write that must take place to free a filled buffer so that it can receive a block that the application program is trying to read. Space Writes occur only when there are no more empty buffers of the appropriate size. In the appropriate subpool the least recently used (LRU) buffer is written out and thus made available. With good selection of the number of subpool buffers, and with good use of Background Writes, Space Writes should be virtually eliminated.

Background Writes (VSAM Only).   Background Writes may be optionally specified as a supplement to Space Writes and Sync Point Writes. Since the application programs must wait anyway for the I/O required to free some buffers, it may be advantageous to take a little more time and free several buffers in each subpool as part of the same operation. When a Background Write is specified, a certain percentage of buffers is also specified. Starting with the LRU buffer in each subpool, that percentage of buffers in *every* subpool are examined, and those buffers that have been altered will be written out. Thus Background Writes can greatly reduce the need for Space Writes.

PERFORMANCE CONSIDERATIONS

The efficiency of buffer pool operations is determined primarily by the number of buffers allocated to each subpool and by the amount of page fixing done. The following sections discuss the interpretation of buffer pool statistics with regard to the sufficiency of the number of buffers. Much of the material in the following two sections is derived from the work of David Schramm (Reference 12).

VSAM Buffer Pool Activity

Activity for each of the VSAM subpools is recorded on Type X'4508' records on the IMS log tape. Several processing programs are available for reading the log tapes and reporting this activity. Although several statistics are recorded, we will limit this discussion to those most pertinent to performance. All of the statistics and indicators discussed in this section are contained in the Type X'4508' log tape records.

A good indication of how busy the buffer pool handlers are is given by the rate of I/O requests. This rate can be broken down to show the amount of keyed requests and the number of RBA requests.

Minimizing physical I/Os implies maximizing the number of DL/I calls satisfied by information already in the buffer pool. One way of doing this is to maximize the number of buffers in each subpool being used. But because having too many buffers can have an adverse impact on space and on paging rates, we try to choose an optimum number of buffers that is normally less than a possible maximum. Thus the issue becomes one of trying to determine if enough buffers have been allocated for efficient operation.

For read activity, a "satisfied in pool" ratio can be obtained by dividing the number of times the requested block was already in the subpool by the total number of read requests. The "satisfied in pool" ratio is intended to give an indication of whether or not there are enough buffers. A low ratio should mean too few buffers. But this ratio must be interpreted in light of the type of processing and the data-base structure, and it is not always a good indicator. For example, random processing of a root-only data base will nearly always yield a low "satisfied in pool" ratio regardless of the number of buffers.

Another indicator is the number of Background Writes. But this parameter indicates the number of times Background Write was invoked, not the number of blocks written.

A further indicator is the number of writes initiated by IMS. This is the number of physical I/Os for Sync Point Writes and Background Writes. Low numbers are desirable.

Perhaps the best indicator is the number of Space Writes issued. If this number is high, there are too few buffers. If it is low, there appears to be enough buffers but it may be that excessive use of Background Write is providing them. If the number of Background Writes is also low, then there are enough buffers in the subpool.

ISAM/OSAM Buffer Pool Activity

ISAM/OSAM buffer pool activity is recorded on Type X'4504' log tape records. These statistics are recorded for the overall buffer pool and not for individual subpools. Again, several processing programs are available for reporting this activity.

As with VSAM, the "satisfied in pool" ratio is generally a good indicator of adequate buffer pool configuration, although it can be misleading for some types of processing and/or data-base structures. This ratio is obtained by dividing the number of requests satisfied from the pool by the sum of the number of calls to the buffer pool manager plus the number of requests for a new logical record.

OSAM is used to write all blocks. It is also used to read OSAM blocks and to reread ISAM blocks forced out of a buffer since the last sync point but that must now be reread. The following statistics, sometimes called the physical I/O profile, give a good indication of ISAM/OSAM buffer pool performance:

- I/O rate
- OSAM reads
- OSAM chained writes
- OSAM forced writes
- ISAM reads

The I/O rate gives a good indication of how much work is being done by the buffer pool handler.

Chained writes occur at program termination or as the result of Sync point or Checkpoint calls. All buffers altered since the last sync point (or checkpoint) or program initiation are chained together and written out by OSAM.

Forced writes occur when a buffer must be freed to receive an incoming block. These are analogous to the VSAM Space Writes. A high number of forced writes indicates an insufficient number of buffers in one or more subpools or inefficient application programming that creates too many I/Os between sync points.

Page-Fixing

The buffer pools are allocated in virtual storage. This means that a given set of buffers may not be in main memory when it is needed. Thus paging I/O can be required in addition to data-base I/O. The paging I/O can be greatly reduced by page-fixing the frequently used buffers in main memory. In VSAM each subpool contains buffers and input/output control blocks (IOBs). Buffers and/or IOBs can be page-fixed. Whichever is chosen is fixed for all subpools. For ISAM/OSAM buffers, buffer prefixes and subpool headers as well as individual subpools can be page-fixed.

BUFFER POOL GUIDELINES

The selection of optimal values for buffer pool parameters is very elusive without the aid of existing buffer pool statistics. If simulation or modeling of I/O activity can be done before implementation, pre-tuning is desirable. Otherwise, tuning based on actual buffer pool statistics after implementation is recommended. Still, the following general design guidelines do apply:

- The size of the buffer pool (ignoring overhead) is the sum of the products of the buffer length times the number of buffers in each subpool.
- The number of subpools and the buffer size in each subpool depends on the block sizes being used.
- The number of buffers in a subpool depends on the amount of I/O activity for blocks of that size.
- Try to specify enough buffers to a subpool so that the "satisfied in pool" ratio is high and the number of non-sync-point writes is low.
- An upper limit to overall buffer pool size occurs when paging is significantly increased.
- Try to avoid many different block sizes among data bases and among data sets within a data base. Fewer subpools permit more buffers per subpool without increasing the overall buffer pool size.
- To reduce contention among programs for subpool space, consider giving high-activity programs exclusive use of a subpool by defining unique block sizes in their data bases.
- Consider page-fixing high activity subpools, prefixes, etc. This will improve I/O performance, but it may have an adverse impact on system paging activity.
- Choose different block sizes for indexes and data so that they will not compete with one another for the same buffer subpool.

14
MISCELLANEOUS PERFORMANCE CONSIDERATIONS

VARIABLE-LENGTH SEGMENTS

While variable-length segments are usually considered awkward to application programming, they can provide a performance improvement. One primary purpose is to combine the data of a set of child segments with the data of a parent segment. With the parent and child data all in one segment, it can be obtained with one access rather than with two. Variable-length segments are also useful when one or more fields contain variable-length information such as a textual description. In this case space is saved by not having to define all segment occurrences to be of maximum length.

On the other hand, updating of variable-length segments can be costly if the length of the segment is increased. Such updates mean that the elongated segments cannot be written back to the exact same physical locations from which they were obtained. To alleviate the potential problems, the data-base administrator can specify a maximum and minimum segment size in the DBD. This makes it more likely that elongated segments will fit conveniently. The maximum segment size is a limiting factor. It should reflect the size of the largest segment to be encountered. The minimum segment size is used for initial space allocation. It must be large enough to contain the entire sequence field of the segment; however, it is recommended that it also be large enough to contain a reasonable majority of complete segments.

In HISAM, when a lengthened segment is rewritten, its logical record is rewritten to acquire needed space. Any displaced segments go into the overflow data set, and additional I/Os will be required to access them. In HDAM and HIDAM, elongated segments go back into their original locations in space is available. If not, the data and prefix portions are split apart, and the data goes into another location and is chained to the prefix. If an update decreases the size of a segment that has been so split, its parts will be put back together if they will fit into the original location.

SYNC POINTS

A sync point is a point of committment in which updated data is considered to be correct, and the updates are actually written to the data base. In message processing programs (MPPs) and transaction-oriented batch message programs (BMPs), updated segments are not written to the data base until the program reaches a sync point, and updated segments are generally not available to other programs until a sync point occurs. Sync points occur at program termination and whenever checkpoint calls are issued. In single-mode MPPs and BMPs, sync points occur automatically when input messages are retrieved from the input queue. In batch programs, sync points are caused only by checkpoints and by program termination.

Application programmers should understand that data-base performance may depend in part on their not delaying sync points unnecessarily.

ENQUEUING AND HOLDING SEGMENTS

In order to guarantee the integrity of the data, it is necessary to impose certain controls on the concurrent use of a data base by two or more programs. One program must not be allowed to modify or destroy data that another program is currently using. Conversely, the integrity of the data must be guaranteed to the program that is using it. Thus the capability must exist for a program to lock a segment or a record that is to be updated so that another program cannot also update the data, and possibly not even read it, until the controlling update is completed and committed. Program isolation and Q command codes provide this capability. It is essential that application programmers be aware of the adverse performance consequences of locking other programs out of segments and records for any longer than necessary.

Program Isolation

With program isolation an entire data-base record can be enqueued and made unavailable to other concurrent programs. There are many situations that justify making the entire record unavailable to other programs while a controlling program performs its functions. The central idea is to guarantee the integrity of the data.

Assuming that two programs are both scheduled and running concurrently, program isolation enqueues and dequeues segments of a data-base record according to the types of calls and the processing options in force. In the current release of IMS/VS, four levels of enqueue are available, as follows:

- Level 1—Get Only (process option GO).
- Level 2—Get (process option G).
- Level 3—Update (process option I, R, D, A).
- Level 4—Exclusive (process option E).

A GET function with a process option of G means that the application program wants to retrieve a segment containing committed data—that is, data that is considered correct and that can be reconstructed if a rollback is necessary. In this case a Level-2 enqueue is placed on every segment in the data-base record, and it remains in effect until the application program moves to another data-base record (or until checkpoint or program termination).

By contrast, a GET function with a process option of GO means that an application program does not want to wait until a segment is dequeued to look at it. The program is willing to take a chance on uncommitted, and possibly erroneous, data. In all such cases, immediate access is granted.

When a REPL, DLET, or ISRT call is issued, a Level 3 enqueue is placed on the updated segment. All other segments of the data-base record receive a Level-2 enqueue (which they already have in the case of a REPL or DLET). As soon as the application program moves to another data-base record, the Level-2 enqueues are removed, and those segments become immediately available to other programs. But the updated segment remains unavailable with its Level-3 enqueue until a sync point is created either by a checkpoint call or by program termination.

When a segment is accessed with a process option of E, the entire data-base record is enqueued at Level 4, and its segments are unavailable to other programs (except to those that want to do a Get Only with process option GO) until a sync point occurs.

Q Command Code

The Q command code may be used by MPPs and BMPs to enqueue certain segments so that other programs cannot update them. If the controlling program does no updates on these segments, they may be released by an operating system DEQ action or by a sync point. If updated, these segments can be released only by a sync point.

Get Hold Calls

While it is true that a Get Hold call must preceed a Replace or a Delete call, it is not true that the Get Hold places an update (Level-3) enqueue on the subject segment. The Get and the Get Hold calls both place Level-2 enqueues on the segment, and it is the update call itself that raises the enqueue level to Level 3.

Application programs are sometimes written to issue a Get Unique early in the program, followed by processing, and then followed by a Get Hold in order to initiate the update process. The erroneous supposition is that between the Get Unique and the Get Hold, the segment is available to other programs, and that it is the Get Hold that enqueues it for update. Thus a DL/I call is wasted by not realizing that any kind of Get (except for process option GO) enqueues at Level 2, and it is the update call itself that enqueues at Level 3.

Data Sharing

Data sharing has come to mean the sharing of a data base by two or more IMS (or other) systems residing in the same processor or in different processors. Such sharing is policed by a Data Base Recovery Control (DBRC) subsystem, an IMS/VS Resource Lock Manager (IRLM) subsystem, and a Recovery Control (RECON) data set. A description of data sharing is beyond the scope of this book. We will mention briefly, however, that there are two levels of control: (1) data base level sharing and (2) block level sharing. In data base level sharing, the entire data base is unavailable to any other registered user until released by the controlling program. In block level sharing, two or more programs can access the same data base, and the IRLM subsystem is used to give the same enqueue and dequeue protection as program isolation. Again, good performance can depend on wise use by the application programmer.

DEVICE SHARING

The physical placement of data bases on channels and devices is of major importance for performance. The expected performance benefits of a well-designed data base may never be realized if the application program must continuously wait for a channel or a device to become available for the desired I/O operations.

Channel/Device Busy

If a physical I/O is requested that requires a channel or a device that happens to be busy at the time, the requested I/O must necessarily wait until the required resource becomes free. The guideline is to distribute the physical placement of data bases so that those data bases that are expected to be in use at the same time are placed on different channels, if possible, and certainly on different devices. This is of most importance during peak periods when avoiding unnecessary delays is most critical. Highest priority should be given to the placement of data bases that are used together during peak periods for high volume transactions. The importance of physical placement of the data bases cannot be overemphasized.

Access Arm Movement

A related problem of device sharing is access arm contention. If a number of application functions are using data bases on the same device, and each function requires movement of the access arm to its own set of cylinders, considerable time can be wasted. The mechanical movement of the access arm is frequently the largest single time-delay factor of physical I/O.

To illustrate this consideration, consider three programs accessing data on three sets of cylinders, as depicted in Figure 14-1. If Pro-

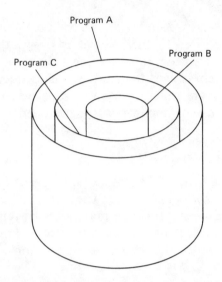

Figure 14–1. Device sharing by cylinders.

gram A were the only program running, then it could move the access arm to its own set of cylinders and keep it there without any further significant movement. If Programs A and B are running at the same time, then Program B may move the access arm to its cylinders and Program A will have to move it back again for its next I/O. While a third program may not increase the distance the arm must move, it will increase the frequency of movement. The more programs we have running at the same time, the greater the likelihood the arm has been moved and will have to be moved back. But if these programs are accessing data on different devices, the problem of arm movement vanishes.

15
APPLICATION PROGRAM DESIGN GUIDELINES

INTRODUCTION

Not infrequently, the real culprit in a poorly performing data-base system is a poorly designed application program rather than the data base itself. There are usually many different ways in which a data base may be accessed in order to satisfy an external functional requirement. Each of these accessing strategies will be referred to as a *call pattern*. For any given situation, some call patterns will perform more efficiently than others. The proper choice depends not only on the function being performed but also on the design of the data base and on the distribution patterns of its segments.

EFFICIENT CALL PATTERNS

Call-pattern efficiency must be considered from at least three perspectives:

1. The effect of environment variations on call patterns.
2. Call pattern alternatives within a given environment.
3. Proper call type to access a given segment.

We will consider each perspective in turn.

The Effect of Environment Variations on Call Patterns

As a simple example of DL/I call-pattern efficiency in varying environments, consider the following functional requirement. For a given set of key values, we want to update the root segments containing those keys. In cases where a root segment does not exist for a given key, we want to create and insert a root segment.

The call pattern that seems most natural is depicted in Figure 15–1. This call pattern begins with a GET UNIQUE followed, if successful, by a REPLACE. If the GET UNIQUE results in a "not found" status, it is followed by an INSERT.

Another approach which performs the same function is depicted in Figure 15–2. This call pattern begins with an INSERT. If the resulting status code reveals that the segment already exists, then a GET UNIQUE followed by a REPLACE is performed. While at first glance this approach may appear more awkward than the first call pattern, it will be shown that under certain environments it can be more efficient.

Let's consider two cases. Case 1 represents a fairly steady-state environment in which the required root segment will be found 80 percent of the time. Case 2, on the other hand, represents a growth situation in which the required segment will already exist only 20 percent of the time. Assume that 100 keys are to be processed. Figure

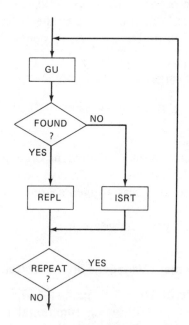

Figure 15–1. Call pattern no. 1.

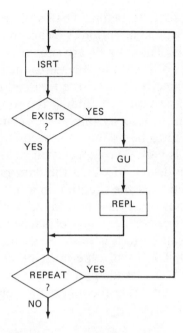

Figure 15–2. Call pattern no. 2.

15-3 shows the number of DL/I calls to be executed for each call pattern and case.

To be rigorous, we should consider that different amounts of time may be required to perform the different call types. We normally assume the same amount of time for a Replace as for a Get. But Inserts usually take somewhat longer. For simplicity in this discussion, we will assume the same amount of time for each of the three

		CASE 1	CASE 2
CALL PATTERN 1	GU	100	100
	REPL	80	20
	ISRT	20	80
CALL PATTERN 2	GU	80	20
	REPL	80	20
	ISRT	100	100

Figure 15–3. Number of DL/I calls executed for two different call patterns.

call types, and the points to be made can still be illustrated. On the basis of this simplifying assumption, we can now talk merely of the total number of calls. These totals are shown in Figure 15–4.

Plotting the results of Figure 15–4 leads to the graph of Figure 15–5. This shows that the efficiency of the first call pattern is relatively invariant with the expectation of finding the root, while the second pattern is directly influenced by this expectation. If only a few of the roots are expected to be present, the second pattern is superior. Otherwise, the first is best. The expectation of finding the root can be a function of the degree to which the data base is loaded, or it can simply be a function of the situation in a fully loaded data base.

Figure 15–5 demonstrates the importance of the environment as well as the call pattern for accessing efficiency. To be rigorous in determining which call pattern is more efficient, the expected time for performing each DL/I call type must be considered, and this depends largely on the access method being used. If the data base is indexed, the time for updating the index must also be added to the times of successful INSERTs.

Call Pattern Alternatives Within a Given Environment

In this section we will demonstrate that for a given function and a given data-base environment, several alternative call patterns can be considered, and that some of these call patterns will perform more efficiently than others. Consider the logically related data bases shown in Figure 15–6. A logical child segment, ENROLLED, is used to show the enrollment of a student in a course offering. Another logical child segment, TAKEN, is used to show which courses the

	CASE 1	CASE 2
CALL PATTERN 1	200	200
CALL PATTERN 2	260	140

Figure 15–4. Summary of DL/I calls executed for two different call patterns.

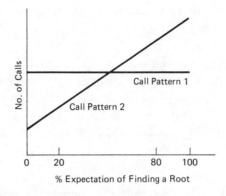

Figure 15–5. Effect of environment on call-pattern efficiency.

student has previously taken. In addition, a recursive logical relationship exists between the COURSE and PREREQUISITE segments. We will consider two different situations applied to this database environment.

As a simple first example, assume that we are positioned at a particular TAKEN segment for a student and we want to find all the other students who have taken the same course. There are several ways we could proceed. One approach is to return to the first TAKEN segment, do a series of qualified Get Nexts on TAKEN segments for the given COURSE, and identify the students by examining the concatenated key in the Program Control Block (PCB) after retrieving each qualifying TAKEN segment. Another approach would be to scan all STUDENT segments and query their TAKEN segments to see if any is for the specified course. For any environment, this last approach appears to be inferior to the first.

Of course, if we include logical relations or secondary indexes, additional approaches become available. The data-base administra-

Figure 15–6. STUDENT–COURSE data base.

tor or the application programmer must be able to estimate the amount of work required by each alternative in order to select the most efficient approach.

For a second example suppose the task at hand is to enroll a student in a given course if (1) the student has not already taken the course with a passing grade and (2) the student has taken all the prerequisites for the course with passing grades. There are several DL/I call patterns that could be used for this function. We will examine two of them.

Call Pattern No. 1.   For the course in which the student wants to enroll, the TAKEN segments can be scanned to see if the student has previously taken the course with a passing grade. Then for each prerequisite, the TAKEN segments can be rescanned to see if the student has successfully taken them. If there are three prerequisites, there will be four complete scans of the TAKEN segments.

Call Pattern No. 2.   We are justified in assuming that there are a relatively small number of prerequisites, and that for any given course, its prerequisites are few enough to be contained in a main memory table. This table can be built with only one scan of the course's PREREQ segments. By using this table and by scanning the TAKEN segments one time, the program can check to see if credit already exists for the course in which the student wants to enroll and if the prerequisites have been met.

In this approach we have a single scan of the PREREQ segments and a single scan of the TAKEN segments as opposed to a scan of the TAKEN segments to check prior credit plus an additional scan of the TAKEN segments for each prerequisite to be checked.

In each of the two examples just cited, the more efficient call pattern was rather obvious. But more often than not, the proper choice is not obvious. In such situations, the simulation and modeling techniques to be presented in Chapters 17 and 18 can be used, before writing the application program, to determine the most efficient call patterns for the situation at hand.

Proper Call Type for Accessing a Given Segment

Frequently there are several ways of accessing a given segment, and a proper choice must consider related program requirements and also how DL/I functions internally. Other considerations are such things as the distance of the segment from the current position, the parentage setting, and the amount of qualifying to be done. The application programmer should always be aware of, and give consideration to, these items.

As examples, should a qualified Get Next or Get Unique be used to access a particular segment located beyond the current position? Should a qualified call be used when an unqualified call will yield the same results? When should command codes such as F and L be used, and when should they not be used?

To make proper choices one must know something of IMS's internal processing. For example, a Get Next begins its search from the current position, while a Get Unique locates (or re-locates) the root and works its way downward. And while a qualified call may be a safer approach, an unqualified call for the same segment requires less work by IMS.

PRESCRIBED I/O STANDARDS

In some installations, the data-base administrator who designs and establishes the data base will also review the application program requirements and establish performance criteria that the program will be expected to meet. Such parameters as the number and types of DL/I calls and the average expected times for the DL/I calls are established as further program requirements. Program reviews and actual performance tests are made at stages throughout the development cycle, and programs failing to meet their performance standards are thoroughly reviewed and redesigned if at all possible.

ACCESSING ACROSS LOGICAL BOUNDARIES

The application program should avoid, as much as possible, accessing across logical boundaries. When a logical child segment is accessed, two different concatenated keys are made available to the application program. One concatenated key, in the key feedback area of the PCB mask, defines the path to the logical child via its physical parent (or what would have been its physical parent if physical pairing had been used). The other concatenated key, in the application program's I/O area, defines the path to the logical child via its destination parent. Thus the identity of all segments in both paths is made known to the application program just by accessing the logical child segment itself (not concatenated with its destination parent). Frequently knowing just these key values is enough. The only reason for an application program to deliberately access the destination parent or its higher-level parents is when the non-key contents of these segments are also required.

ACCESSING GUIDELINES

The following guidelines are suggested as a means of obtaining greater application program efficiency with regard to data-base operations. While many other guidelines of interest to the data-base administrator could be cited (and are cited elsewhere in this book), the ones below are selected as being of interest to the application programmer.

Reduce the Number of DL/I Calls

- *Use path calls.* Whenever segments on different levels of the same path are needed, consider retrieving them using one DL/I path call.
- *Use other command codes.* A major purpose of command codes is to vary the effects of positioning or to alter other normal effects of DL/I calls without using additional calls to produce those variations.
- *Use parallel processing.* By maintaining several positions on the data base, the necessity of issuing GU calls just to reestablish position can be greatly reduced.
- *Avoid searching a twin chain more than once.* Searching long twin chains can be very costly. If a search must be made, then if segments are encountered that contain information that will also be needed later, extract such information and store it in tables for later use.

- *Avoid retrieving the same segment more than once.* The same comment as in the preceding item applies.
- *Use qualified SSAs to find a particular segment.* It is faster for DL/I to search for the segment than for the application program to search by issuing a series of Get Next calls and testing the keys that are returned.
- *When inserting, use a qualified SSA for each higher level segment if not already positioned under the appropriate parentage.* This avoids the necessity of issuing prior Get calls for positioning and to verify the existence of the needed parents. If the Insert fails because a parent is missing, the missing parent can be identified by examining the PCB status code and key feedback area. On the other hand, if positioning is already established, SSAs for the higher-level segments need not be used.
- *After accessing a dependent segment, if the keys of its parents are needed, get them from the PCB.* There is no need to access the parents to get their key values since their keys are already available in the PCB. The parents need be accessed only in non-key information is needed from them.
- *After accessing a logical child, if the keys of its destination parentage are needed, get them from the logical child's concatenated key.* The destination parents need be accessed only if non-key information is needed from them.

Minimize the Search Path for Each DL/I Call

- *Try to avoid searching long twin chains.* Long twin chains pose one of the biggest problems of data-base performance. Processing their segment occurrences in a sequential or skip-sequential mode may be appropriate, but try to avoid searching a long twin chain just to locate a small number of segments. This is especially true for logical twin chains.
- *Try to access logical children through their physical parents.* Avoid crossing logical boundaries as much as possible.
- *Take advantage of positioning.* Use a call that will follow the shortest path to the desired segment.
- *Use command codes F & L for retrieves.* When supported by the appropriate pointer options, these command codes enable DL/I to go directly to first or last segment on a twin chain.

Their use can save much internal searching since the twin chain does not have to be scanned. This is especially true for logical twin chains.

- *Insert first or last on twin chains.* If key sequence is not important, inserts to the first or last positions on the twin chain can be accomplished without searching the twin chain.

Use Simple DL/I Calls

- *Don't overqualify.* Each qualified SSA requires additional DL/I processing. Take advantage of positioning as much as possible.
- *Use a boolean SSA only if it saves additional DL/I calls.* Boolean SSAs also require additional DL/I processing.

Release Enqueued Segments as Quickly as Possible

- *Dequeue nonupdated segments.* Move to the next data-base record as quickly as possible.
- *Dequeue updated segments.* Consider issuing a checkpoint if considerable processing remains after data-base activity.
- *Avoid enqueues.* Use the Get Only process option whenever possible consistent with the requirement for integrity.

PART V
PREDICTING DATA-BASE
PERFORMANCE

16
SPACE CALCULATIONS

INTRODUCTION

One of the major aspects of physical design is estimating the amount of storage space that will be required to hold the data base. It is also a very tedious exercise if done manually. Not only are the calculations laborious, but obtaining some of the starting parameters such as the sizes of the segment prefixes and the amount of overhead in a block can be difficult to accomplish. Fortunately, at least in the case of DL/I data bases, programs are available to make these determinations and to perform these calculations. Therefore the material in this chapter is included to explain the concepts of space calculations rather than to encourage the designer to do it manually. The designer is strongly urged to use the automated tools that are available, and to use the concepts herein presented to understand and to check the reasonableness of the results of these tools.

INPUT FOR SPACE CALCULATIONS

The input data required for automated space calculations consists simply of the information normally contained in the DBD source statements plus certain additional information about segment distributions that can be included with the DBD source statements.

From the DBD statements we use the names and lengths of the segments, their physical and logical relationships to each other, and their average frequencies of occurrence. The frequencies specified in the DBD are simply the single-valued average number of segments per parent, or per data base in the case of the root. More precise space calculations are made possible by augmenting the DBD information with the expected frequency distributions of the segments.

The more commonly used distributions are the Poisson, Uniform, Bernoulli, and the 80–20 rule. Others are also occasionally specified. When going to this degree of sophistication, provision should be made for the designer to use any other distributions that apply more appropriately. For example, the presence or absence of a segment may depend on the presence or absence of some other "controlling" segment. Provision should be made for such situations. For simplicity in the examples to be presented, we will deal simply with average numbers of segment occurrences and not with individual segment-type distributions.

SUBTREES

The notion of subtrees will be introduced at this point as a convenient technique to use when calculating data-base sizes. A subtree of segment type X is defined to be one occurrence of segment type X plus the collection of all segment occurrences that are hierarchically subservient to that occurrence of segment X. Each segment occurrence that has children defines a proper subtree. Each segment occurrence without children defines a trivial subtree consisting of only that segment occurrence.

In Figure 16–1, occurrences of segment types C, D, and F are trivial subtrees because they are the low-level segments on their respective paths. The subtree of B1 is composed of segments B1, C1, C2, and D1. The subtree of B2 comprises segments B2, C3, D2, and D3. E1 and E3 are also trivial subtrees. E2's subtree contains E2 and F1.

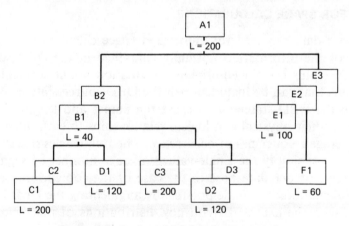

Figure 16–1. A typical data-base record.

A1's subtree is A1 plus the collection of all the B, C, D, E, and F type segments subservient to A1. For purposes of calculation, it is convenient to think of a subtree as containing a defining segment occurrence plus the subtrees of all immediate dependents of that segment.

Calculating Subtree Length

The length of the subtree of a segment is merely the length of the defining segment plus the lengths of all its dependent subtrees. But it is impractical, and usually impossible, to determine the exact number of occurrences of the dependent segment types, because the number of occurrences varies from record to record, and it also varies dynamically within a record as insertions and deletions are made during processing. Hence we calculate a segment's subtree size on the basis of an "average" record by estimating the expected number of occurrences of each subservient segment type.

For space estimates, maximum values are sometimes used rather than average values for segment occurrence expectations. However, more realistic space estimates can be obtained by using statistical expectations, when known, for the number of segment occurrences. In the examples that follow, F represents the average expected frequency of occurrence of each segment type, and L represents the segment length.

A DL/I segment contains both a prefix and data. The prefix contains pointers and status information, and its length depends on the storage organization (HD or HS), and if HD, on the selected pointer options. In manual space calculations, the prefix size must be calculated. It consists of two bytes (segment code and delete byte) plus four bytes for each pointer to be included. In automated space calculations, the prefix size can automatically be determined according to the pointer options specified in the PCB. For simplicity in the examples to follow, we will assume overall segment lengths without giving detailed consideration to prefix sizes.

Subtree Sizes Without Data Set Groups

For the initial example, assume the data set is not divided into groups. Assume 10,000 occurrences of the root segment A, and assume an "average" data-base record as depicted in Figure 16–2, with segment

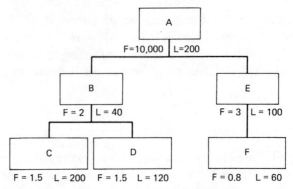

Figure 16-2. Example of an average data-base record.

frequencies (F) and lengths (L) as indicated. (The record depicted in Figure 16-1 can be considered an actual record from this data base.)

The length calculations proceed in the following manner where L(X), S(X), and F(X) represent the length of segment type X (i.e., prefix plus data), the length of the subtree of segment type X, and the average frequency of occurrence of segment type X, respectively.

$$
\begin{aligned}
S(F) &= L(F) = 60 \text{ bytes} \\
S(E) &= L(E) + S(F) \times F(F) \\
     &= 100 + 60 \times 0.8 = 148 \text{ bytes} \\
S(D) &= L(D) = 120 \text{ bytes} \\
S(C) &= L(C) = 200 \text{ bytes} \\
S(B) &= L(B) + S(C) \times F(C) + S(D) \times F(D) \\
     &= 40 + 200 \times 1.5 + 120 \times 1.5 = 520 \text{ bytes} \\
S(A) &= L(A) + S(B) \times F(B) + S(E) \times F(E) \\
     &= 200 + 520 \times 2 + 148 \times 3 = 1{,}684 \text{ bytes}
\end{aligned}
$$

Thus the expected length of a record (an occurrence of the root A and all its dependents) is 1684 bytes. The total number of bytes (TB) for the data base is:

$$
\begin{aligned}
TB &= S(A) \times F(A) \\
   &= 1{,}684 \times 10{,}000 \\
   &= 16{,}840{,}000 \text{ bytes}
\end{aligned}
$$

Subtree Sizes With Data Set Groups

If the data base is divided into data set groups, the space calculations must be performed on a per-group basis, as each group will be defined to the system as a separate data set having its own storage characteristics. In the following example we will arbitrarily assign segment types A, B, and C to the primary data set group; segment type D to a secondary data set group; and segment types E and F to another secondary data set group. In Figure 16–3 the numbers inside the segments indicate the group to which that segment type is assigned.

The space calculations for each group are performed as follows:

Group 1.

$$S(C1) = L(C) = 200 \text{ bytes}$$

$$S(B1) = L(B) + S(C1) \times F(C)$$
$$= 40 + 200 \times 1.5 = 340 \text{ bytes}$$

$$S(A1) = L(A) + S(B1) \times F(B)$$
$$= 200 + 340 \times 2 = 880 \text{ bytes}$$

$$TB(1) = S(A1) \times F(A)$$
$$= 880 \times 10,000 = 8,800,000 \text{ bytes}$$

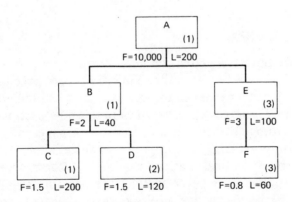

Figure 16–3. Example of an average data-base record divided into data set groups.

Group 2.

$$S(D2) = L(D) = 120 \text{ bytes}$$
$$S(B2) = S(D2) \times F(D)$$
$$= 120 \times 1.5 = 180 \text{ bytes}$$
$$S(A2) = S(B2) \times F(B)$$
$$= 180 \times 2 = 360 \text{ bytes}$$
$$TB(2) = S(A2) \times F(A)$$
$$= 360 \times 10{,}000 = 3{,}600{,}000 \text{ bytes}$$

Group 3.

$$S(F3) = L(F) = 60 \text{ bytes}$$
$$S(E3) = L(E) + S(F3) \times L(F)$$
$$= 100 + 60 \times 0.8 = 148 \text{ bytes}$$
$$S(A3) = S(E3) \times F(E)$$
$$= 148 \times 3 = 444 \text{ bytes}$$
$$TB(3) = S(A3) \times F(A)$$
$$= 444 \times 10{,}000 = 4{,}440{,}000 \text{ bytes}$$

Total for Data Base.   The total number of bytes for the data base is the sum of the sizes of the data set groups:

$$TB = TB(1) + TB(2) + TB(3)$$
$$= 8{,}800{,}000 + 3{,}600{,}000 + 4{,}440{,}000$$
$$= 16{,}840{,}000 \text{ bytes}$$

REQUIRED DISK SPACE

Although we have calculated the number of segment bytes in each data base (or data set group), the required storage space necessitates additional considerations leading to even larger numbers. To calculate required storage space, we have to consider such variables as the type of storage device, track capacity, access method, block size (or control interval size), and desired free space.

To understand the calculations that follow, the reader must remember that blocks are never completely filled with segment bytes. While loading segments into a block, there is usually some waste space resulting from not having enough room to accommodate the next segment. Intended free space can also be specified to accommodate future inserts. In addition and depending on the access method used, each block contains a number of overhead fields such as Free Space Elements (FSEs), Root Anchor Points (RAPs), Control Interval Definition Fields (CIDFs), Record Definition Fields (RDFs), and others. Although Figure 16-4 shows the overhead grouped at the beginning of the block for simplicity, some of it is actually distributed throughout the block.

Free space can be provided in HD organizations to allow for database expansion as new segments are inserted during actual processing. To provide for expansion, the designer can designate the percentage of space within a block to be left empty when the data base is loaded or reorganized. The designer can also designate a number of blocks distributed through the data base to be left entirely empty. Thus the number of bytes required for storing a data base depends not only on the number of segment bytes to be stored, but also on the overhead fields, the end of block waste, the free space within the blocks, and the number of initially empty blocks. The basic calculations for estimating storage space follow.

Basic Calculations

The total number of storage bytes required for the data base is given by:

$$TSS = NB \times BLKSZ \tag{1}$$

where:

TSS = total storage space in bytes
NB = number of required blocks (to be calculated)
$BLKSZ$ = block size in bytes

Overhead	Segment 1	Segment 2	. . .	Segment n	EOB Waste

Figure 16-4. Overhead and segment storage in a typical block.

The number of required blocks (NB) is given by:

$$NB = \left. \frac{TB}{EFFBLK \times (1-FSB)} \right| \text{(next-highest integer)}^{(2)}$$

where:

$$TB = \text{total number of segment bytes}$$
$$EFFBLK = \text{effective block size in bytes}$$
$$FSB = \text{percentage of entire blocks to remain empty}$$

The EFFBLK is the number of segment bytes to be stored in a block. This is given by:

$$EFFBLK = (BLKSZ) \times (1-FSW) - OVHD - EOBW \quad (3)$$

where:

$$FSW = \text{percentage of free Space within the blocks}$$
$$OVHD = \text{block overhead (RAP, FSE, CIDF, RDF, etc.) in bytes (to be estimated)}$$
$$EOBW = \text{End of block waste in bytes (to be calculated)}$$

The calculation of EOBW, which can be complex, is explained in the next section. Comments on estimating the overhead will be presented later.

End of Block Waste

There is some waste space at the end of a HSAM or a HIDAM block whenever the next segment is too large to fit into the remaining space. But for HISAM or HDAM data bases, the expected waste space should be calculated on a logical record or slot basis, and the result should be multiplied by the number of logical records or slots per block. On a block basis, the derivation of the waste space calculation follows.

Consider the following probability distribution for segment lengths in the data base:

Length in Bytes	Probability of Occurrence
1	p_1
2	p_2
3	p_3
.	.
.	.
.	.
n	p_n

The expected segment length, E(L), is given by:

$$E(L) = 1 \times p_1 + 2 \times p_2 + 3 \times p_3 + \ldots + n \times p_n$$

The longer the segment, the larger the probability of its being the one that does not fit into the remaining space in the block. The probability distribution for the length of the segment that does not fit is given by:

Length in Bytes	Probability of Occurrence
1	$p_1 \times 1/E(L)$
2	$p_2 \times 2/E(L)$
3	$p_3 \times 3/E(L)$
.	.
.	.
.	.
n	$p_n \times n/E(L)$

The expected length, $E(L')$, of this nonfitting segment is:

$$E(L') = 1 \times p_1 \times 1/E(L) + 2 \times p_2 \times 2/E(L) + \ldots + n \times p_n \times n/E(L)$$

$$= \frac{1}{E(L)} (1^2 \times p_1 + 2^2 \times p_2 + \ldots + n^2 \times p_n)$$

$$= \frac{E(L^2)}{E(L)}$$

For a nonfitting segment of length L', the probability distribution for the size of the EOBW space is:

Length in Bytes	Probability of Occurrence
1	$1/L'$
2	$1/L'$
3	$1/L'$
.	.
.	.
.	.
$L'-1$	$1/L'$

Thus for a given nonfitting segment size, L', the expected amount of end of block waste, $E(W/L')$, is calculated as follows:

$$E(W|L') = 1 \times 1/L' + 2 \times 1/L' + \ldots + (L'-1) \times 1/L'$$

$$= (1/L') \times (1 + 2 + 3 + \ldots + (L'-1))$$

$$= \frac{1}{L'} \times \frac{(L'-1) \times L'}{2}$$

$$= \frac{L'-1}{2}$$

The resulting expected waste, E(W), considering all segment sizes, is as follows:

$$E(W) = E(E(W|L')) = \frac{E(L')}{2} - \frac{1}{2}$$

$$= \frac{E(L^2)}{2 \times E(L)} - \frac{1}{2}$$

Thus:

$$EOBW = E(W) = \frac{E(L^2)}{2 \times E(L)} - \frac{1}{2}$$

Example

We will use the logical model of Figure 16–2 to illustrate the space calculations, and for simplicity we will assume it is not to be divided into data set groups. If the data base is divided into groups, separate space calculations must be performed for each data set group.

We have already determined that the total bytes (TB) is 16,840,000 bytes. Assume a block size of 2048 bytes. To allow for future expansion, assume free space allowances of 10 percent for FSW and 20 percent for FSB. These parameters are appropriate for HIDAM data bases. In HISAM there are no free space parameters, and in HDAM free space in the root addressable area is generally counterproductive. The calculations to follow can apply to HISAM logical records as well as to HDAM blocks simply by setting FSB and FSW to zero.

We first calculate the estimated EOBW. This is done on the basis of a single root segment and its average subtree. The probability distribution of segment length, L, and its square, L2, are given by the following:

Segment	L	L2	Probability
A	200	40,000	1/14.4
B	40	1,600	2/14.4
C	200	40,000	3/14.4

Segment	L	L^2	Probability
D	120	14,400	3/14.4
E	100	10,000	3/14.4
F	60	3,600	2.4/14.4

where the probabilities are obtained by counting the total number of occurrences of each segment type in the average data-base record. The expected segment length is:

$$
\begin{aligned}
E(L) &= 200 \times 1/14.4 + 40 \times 2/14.4 + 200 \times 3/14.4 \\
&\quad + 120 \times 3/14.4 + 100 \times 3/14.4 + 60 \times 2.4/14.4 \\
&= (1/14.4) \times (200 \times 1 + 40 \times 2 + 200 \times 3 + 120 \\
&\quad \times 3 + 100 \times 3 + 60 \times 2.4) \\
&= (1/14.4) \times 1,684
\end{aligned}
$$

Similarly, the expectation of the squared segment length, L2, is:

$$
\begin{aligned}
E(L2) &= 40,000 \times 1/14.4 + 1,600 \times 2/14 + 40,000 \\
&\quad \times 3/14.4 + 14,400 \times 3/14.4 + 10,000 \times 3/14.4 \\
&\quad + 3,600 \times 2.4/14.4 \\
&= (1/14.4) \times (40,000 \times 1 + 1,600 \times 2 + 40,000 \\
&\quad \times 3 + 14,400 \times 3 + 10,000 \times 3 + 3,600 \times 2.4) \\
&= (1/14.4) \times 245,040.
\end{aligned}
$$

Finally, the EOBW is given by:

$$
\begin{aligned}
EOBW &= \frac{E(L2)}{2 \times E(L)} - \frac{1}{2} \\[2mm]
&= \frac{(1/14.4) \times 245,040}{2 \times (1/14.4) \times 1,684} - \frac{1}{2} \\[2mm]
&= \frac{245,040}{3,368} - \frac{1}{2} \\[2mm]
&= 72.3 \text{ bytes}
\end{aligned}
$$

The effective block size (EFFBLK) can now be calculated. For this example, we will arbitrarily assume 31 bytes of overhead. The actual amount of overhead depends on the DL/I access method, the system access method (VSAM or ISAM/OSAM), and certain internal factors (FSEs, number of overflow pointers, and so on). For simplicity, we will assume a collective overhead of 31 bytes. The effective block size is as follows:

$$EFFBLK = BLKSZ \times (1-FSW) - OVHD - EOBW$$
$$= 2{,}048 \times (1-.10) - 31 - 72.3$$
$$= 1{,}740 \text{ bytes}$$

The required number of blocks, NB, is:

$$NB = \frac{TB}{EFFBLK \times (1-FSB)}$$

$$NB = \frac{16{,}840{,}000}{1{,}740 \times (1-.20)}$$

$$= 12{,}098 \text{ blocks}$$

The total storage required for storing the 16,840,000-byte data base can now be given by:

$$TSS = NB \times BLKSZ$$
$$= 12{,}098 \times 2{,}048$$
$$= 24{,}776{,}704 \text{ bytes}$$

But if the data base grows to fill the free space initially set aside, this same storage space can accommodate up to 23,520,000 bytes.

ON ESTIMATING OVERHEAD

When estimating the amount of overhead (OVHD) to be used in equation 3 given earlier in the chapter, we have to consider the overhead inherent in VSAM itself and also the overhead associated with DL/I's use of VSAM. The Virtual Sequential Access Method (VSAM) is the only operating system access method we will consider in this context.

The VSAM overhead consists of one or two record definition fields (RDF) and a control interval definition field (CIDF). This type of overhead amounts to seven bytes per control interval (block) for the HSAM, HDAM, and HIDAM access methods. For HISAM the VSAM overhead is also seven bytes if there is only one logical record per block (a rare case); otherwise, it is ten bytes.

The overhead due to DL/I's use of VSAM is more elusive. It consists of free space pointers and length fields (HIDAM and HDAM), root anchor points (HDAM), logical record pointers (HISAM), and other indicators. Its estimation depends heavily on the access method being used, and the total amount of such overhead depends primarily on the number of free space elements, the number of root anchor points, or the number of logical records as the case may be. Its value ranges upward from a minimum of four bytes. A range of 30 to 60 bytes is not unreasonable.

17
TIME CALCULATIONS

INTRODUCTION

In this chapter we will use analytic calculations to estimate I/O timings for a data-base design. Bear in mind that these calculations are intended for the data-base design process before the data base is actually implemented. The purpose of this exercise is to narrow the number of candidate designs by quickly estimating "ballpark" times for I/O operations. More precise modeling using actual hardware and DL/I calls can then be used to select the best of the remaining designs. Experience indicates this to be a feasible and useful approach to preliminary performance evaluation.

There is a threefold purpose for presenting the material in this chapter. The first reason is to indicate the kind of thinking—the concepts and considerations—that must be addressed in doing a preliminary performance evaluation of a data base and its use. Secondly, we wish to show that the performance estimates, which consist of analytic calculations and some simulation, can be obtained on a computer with greater accuracy and thoroughness than is normally the case with manual techniques. And thirdly, we wish to show that the analytic calculations, at best, are inherently limited in their accuracy. After they have served their purpose, more precise evaluations of the remaining designs requires modeling in a real system environment.

We begin by deriving the probabilities of a physical I/O for three basic types of I/O operations in DL/I. We will then indicate how to combine these probabilities with DL/I call patterns, DL/I path lengths, and hardware characteristics, to produce a timing analysis of the data base as it will be used.

PROBABILITIES OF I/O

Many simplifying assumptions are made in the derivations to follow. All data-base records can be different, and with insertion and deletion activity they can vary dynamically with processing. Therefore the I/O probabilities are derived on the basis of the "average" data-base record. The larger the data base and the larger the number of I/Os, the more reliable we can expect these estimates to be. Some additional simplifying assumptions will be explained as they are encountered in the ensuing derivations.

More precise estimates of I/O probabilities can be obtained by considering the unique probability distributions of each segment type, by working with variances as well as with means, and by considering the special characteristics of the access method being used. Dechow and Lundberg have provided criteria and equations for these more precise estimates (Reference 2).

Types of I/O Probabilities

We will deal with probabilities for three basic types of I/O operations in DL/I. This will be a general treatment, although there are internal variations in the way these operations are performed depending on the access method. The three I/O operations are illustrated in Figure 17-1, and their definitions are as follows:

- PCIO—Parent to Child I/O. The probability of a physical I/O operation in going from a parent segment to the first occurrence of one of its child segment types.
- PTIO—Physical Twin I/O. The probability of a physical I/O operation in going from a segment to its next twin.

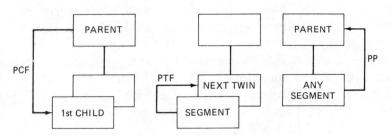

Figure 17-1. Basic types of I/O probabilities.

- PPIO—Physical Parent I/O. The probability of a physical I/O operation in going from a segment to its physical parent.

The calculated probabilities can be presented in tabular form for each segment type as shown in Figure 17-2.

In Figure 17-2, PCIO represents the probability of a physical I/O in going *to* the first occurrence of the named segment *from* its parent; PTIO and PPIO represent the probabilities of a physical I/O in going *from* the named segment *to* to the next twin and to the physical parent, respectively.

Computer assistance in an interactive environment can be quite helpful in calculating these probabilities and in studying how they will vary with changes in block size, free space, access method, and so forth.

The Concept of Distance

Since a block is the unit of information transferred across the I/O channels, the probability that a DL/I call will cause an I/O operation is really the probability that the target segment is in a different block than the source segment at which we are positioned. Thus the determination of an I/O probability is based on further analysis of the segment lengths and storage patterns developed in the previous chapter. (We are ignoring the possibility that the block containing the target segment may already be in the buffer pool from a prior I/O operation.)

The situation is depicted pictorially in Figure 17-3, in which Segment X represents the source segment where we are currently positioned, and Segment Y represents the target segment we wish to access.

SEGMENT	PCIO	PTIO	PPIO
Root	x.xx	x.xx	x.xx
Dep 1	x.xx	x.xx	x.xx
Dep 2	x.xx	x.xx	x.xx
.	.	.	.
.	.	.	.
.	.	.	.

Figure 17-2. Display format for estimated I/O probabilities.

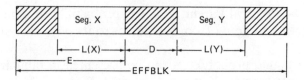

Figure 17-3. Concept of distance between segments.

L(X) and L(Y) represent the segment lengths in bytes. EFFBLK is the effective block size in bytes. E is the distance, in bytes, from the beginning of the block to the end of Segment X, and D is the distance, in bytes, between the end of segment X and the beginning of Segment Y. The inclusive distance between X and Y is denoted by $D(X \rightarrow Y)$ where:

$$D(X \rightarrow Y) = L(X) + D + L(Y)$$

This concept of distance between segments is based on the hierarchical ordering of the segments within the data-base record. To a large extent this hierarchical ordering is present in a newly loaded data base regardless of the DL/I access method. Thus the validity of these analytic time estimates is based on the assumption of a newly loaded data base or at least a data base that is still well-organized.

The general pattern of each of the I/O probabilities with respect to effective block size is depicted in Figure 17-4.

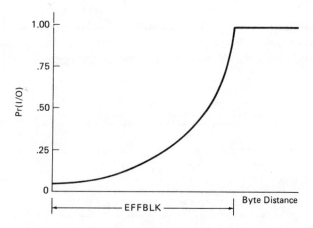

Figure 17-4. Typical I/O probability distribution.

The flat portion of the curve says that if the inclusive distance from the source segment to the target segment exceeds the effective block size (EFFBLK), then there is certainty of a physical I/O operation.

I/O Probability Calculations

Statistically, the segment distribution problem is analogous to the single-server queueing model in which the segments represent customers arriving for service, and the segment lengths represent interarrival times. Assuming that segment X can occur anywhere in the block, E is a random variable with a uniform distribution. Assuming also that the lengths of the segments, as they are encountered in physical storage, are described by the Poisson distribution; and assuming that the target segment, segment Y, is the nth segment following segment X; then the distance, D, between segment X and segment Y is a random variable with a Gamma distribution.

The probability of I/O, Pr(I/O), is the probability that segment X and segment Y are not in the same block. This is given by:

$$Pr(I/O) = Pr(E + D + L(Y) > B)$$

where B is the actual block size.

Without derivation, it is asserted that this probability calculation can reasonably be calculated by:

$$Pr(I/O) = Min \left(1, \frac{D(X \to Y)}{EFFBLK} \right) \qquad (1)$$

where EFFBLK is the effective block size derived in the previous chapter. Equation 1 applies directly to the calculation of I/O probabilities for PCIO and PTIO. The calculations for PPIO, however, are more complex.

The calculation of inclusive distance from a segment (Y) back to its physical parent (X) is complex because we do not know at which occurrence of Y we are positioned. Assuming we are equally likely to be positioned at any occurrence of Y under a parent X, we must calculate the I/O probability from each of the Y occurrences back to X, and then average these probabilities. To do this, we must have some idea of the number of occurrences of Y under X; therefore if the probability distribution of the occurrences of Y is known, the approach is feasible.

The byte distance, D, from the first occurrence of segment Y (Y1) back to its parent, X is given by:

$$D\ (Y1{\rightarrow}X) = D(X{\leftarrow}Y1)$$

The byte distance from the second occurrence of Y (Y2) back to X is given by:

$$D(Y2{\rightarrow}X) = D(X{\rightarrow}Y1) + S(Y)$$

where S(Y) is the average subtree size of Y.

In general, the byte distance from the nth occurrence of Y (Yn) back to its parent X is given by:

$$D(Yn{\rightarrow}X) = D(X{\rightarrow}Y1) + (n\text{-}1) \times S(Y)$$

Applying Equation (1) to the distance from each occurrence of Y back to its parent X, and averaging, we have:

$$PPIO = PPIO(Y1{\rightarrow}X) \times p_1 + PPIO(Y2{\rightarrow}X) \times p_2 + \ldots + PPIO\ (Yn{\rightarrow}X) \times p_n$$

$$= Min\left(1, \frac{D(Y1{\rightarrow}X)}{EFFBLK}\right) \times p_1 + Min\left(1, \frac{D(Y2{\rightarrow}X)}{EFFBLK}\right) \times p_2$$

$$+ \ldots + Min\left(1, \frac{D(Yn{\rightarrow}X)}{EFFBLK}\right) \times p_n \qquad (2)$$

where p_1, p_2, . . . p_n are the probabilities of the existence of the occurrences of segment Y under X.

On the other hand, when working with an "average" data-base record, we must make some simplifying assumptions because we do not know how many actual occurrences of Y may exist for a given parent X. A number of alternatives exist for simplification. The one most commonly used is to calculate the average distance from the Y occurrences back to X and then apply equation 1 directly to this average distance. Using this approach, the following equation approximates the average distance from Y to X:

$$
D(Y \to X) = \frac{1}{F(Y)} \times \begin{bmatrix} D(X \to Y) & + \\ D(X \to Y) + S(Y) & + \\ D(X \to Y) + 2 \times S(Y) & + \\ & \cdot \\ & \cdot \\ & \cdot \\ D(X \to Y) + (F(Y)-1) \times S(Y) & \end{bmatrix}
$$

$$
= \frac{1}{F(Y)} \times \left[F(Y) \times D(X \to Y) + \frac{(F(Y)-1) \times F(Y)}{2} \times S(Y) \right]
$$

$$
= D(X \to Y) + \frac{(F(Y)-1 \times S(Y)}{2} \tag{3}
$$

Equation 1 can now be applied to this average distance to obtain a ballpark I/O probability from a segment to its physical parent.

Special Considerations

These I/O probabilities apply to searching for a desired segment (establishing position) in a DL/I data base. Thus they apply primarily to the GET and GET NEXT family of DL/I calls, and also to INSERT calls. For DELETEs, they apply to the preceding GET HOLD, and they also apply to finding and marking segments dependent to the deleted segment. For REPLACEs they apply to the preceding GET HOLD. To be complete, for INSERTs and DELETEs in HD organizations, we may also want to consider the I/Os involved in accessing the bit maps; and for indexed data bases, the indexes. For all updates we are also concerned with the probability of physical I/Os for output, which in normal operation is the probability that a retrieved block has received one or more updates.

So far we have considered a dichotomous set of probabilities—the probability of one or more I/Os or of no I/Os. For HD organizations this is sufficient, but with HS organizations we might want probability distributions of the exact number of I/Os, as is explained below.

In the HD organization, because of the direct pointers, accesses from one segment to another involve at most one I/O, because the pointers take us directly to the block containing the desired segment. The main time-consuming factor in processing HD data bases is in following long physical or logical twin chains from twin to twin (and from block to block) until finding the desired segment.

In HISAM, which is less frequently used than the HD organizations, the sequential ordering of the search might require more than one physical I/O for a DL/I call. This can be the case when processing twins and skipping past their dependents. It is here that probability distributions for the exact number of I/Os might be desirable. On the other hand, the choice of HISAM is based largely on the concept of processing segments in their hierarchical sequence with a minimum of skipping of intermediate segments. This is to say that with HISAM we will not normally be processing long twin chains unless they are at the lowest level of their respective hierarchical paths.

The foregoing derivations and the example to follow are for probabilities of one or more I/Os per call. These results are valid (except as noted below) for HD organizations and for HISAM as it is normally used.

Finally, the reader is cautioned that there are certain situations to which these probabilities do not apply. They do not apply to HDAM data bases when the source and target segment are both in the Root Addressable Area, because by definition both segments are in the same block. But this consideration is frequently ignored because as the data base is updated and then reorganized, the segment content of the Root Addressable Area changes. These probabilities also do not apply when the source and target segments are not in the same data set group and also when the I/O traverses a logical relationship to another data base. In both cases, there is certainty of an I/O.

I/O Calculation Example

To illustrate the calculation of these I/O probabilities, we use the "average" data-base record depicted in Figure 17-2. This record has segments in the hierarchical order shown in Figure 17-5. The listed frequencies indicate those segments having, on the average, a fractional number of occurrences. Based on this segment pattern, average byte distances for the three basic I/O types are calculated in the sections to follow.

In this example, we assume the HDAM access method with direct access to the root segments. Therefore, the calculations to be illustrated pertain only to processing the data segments. If an indexed access method were being used, the calculation should also include time estimates for searching the index.

Parent to First Occurrence of Each Child.   The inclusive distance from a parent segment (X) to the first occurrence of one of its child segment types (Y) is the length of X plus the length of Y plus the length of the distance (D) between X and Y. The distance is estimated by the product of the frequency and subtree size (S) of each of X's siblings that are to the left of Y. The subtree sizes were calculated in the previous chapter. From Figure 17-5 we calculate the following parent–child distances.

$$
\begin{aligned}
D(A \rightarrow B) &= L(A) + L(B) \\
&= 200 + 40 \\
&= 240 \text{ bytes} \\
D(A \rightarrow E) &= L(A) + F(B) \times S(B) + L(E) \\
&= 200 + 2 \times 520 + 100 \\
&= 1{,}340 \text{ bytes}
\end{aligned}
$$

A	B	C	D	B	C	D	E	F	E	F	E	F

```
L =  200   40  200  120   40  200  120  100   60  100   60  100   60
F =            1.5  1.5        1.5  1.5        .8        .8        .8
```

Figure 17-5. Layout of average data-base record.

$$D(B \rightarrow C) = L(B) + L(C)$$
$$= 40 + 200$$
$$= 240 \text{ bytes}$$
$$D(B \rightarrow D) = L(B) + F(C) \times S(C) + L(D)$$
$$= 40 + 1.5 \times 200 + 120$$
$$= 460 \text{ bytes}$$
$$D(E \rightarrow F) = L(E) + L(F)$$
$$= 100 + 60$$
$$= 160 \text{ bytes}$$

Applying the following equation:

$$Pr(I/O) = \text{Min} \left(1, \frac{D(X \rightarrow Y)}{\text{EFFBLK}} \right) \tag{1}$$

to the distances computed above, we obtain the PCIO probabilities shown in Figure 17-6. In so doing, we are using an EFFBLK of 1740 bytes as calculated in the previous chapter from a 2048-byte block. Note in the table that the PCIO for Segment A is arbitrarily set to one because there is always an I/O in making an initial access to the root segment. And again, the assumption is that all segments are in the same physical data base and in the same data set group.

Segment to Next Twin.   The inclusive distance from a segment occurrence (X) to its next twin (X') is simply the subtree of X plus the gth of X. From the average record in Figure 17-5, we have the following.

$$D(A \rightarrow A') = S(A) + L(A)$$
$$= 1684 + 200$$
$$= 1884 \text{ bytes}$$

Segment	PCIO	PTIO	PPIO
A	1.00		
B	.14		
C	.14		
D	.26		
E	.71		
F	.09		

Figure 17-6. Estimated PCIO probabilities.

$$D(B \rightarrow B') = S(B) + L(B)$$
$$= 520 + 40$$
$$= 560 \text{ bytes}$$
$$D(C \rightarrow C') = S(C) + L(C)$$
$$= 200 + 200$$
$$= 400 \text{ bytes}$$
$$D(D \rightarrow D') = S(D) + L(D)$$
$$= 120 + 120$$
$$= 240 \text{ bytes}$$
$$D(E \rightarrow E') = S(E) + L(E)$$
$$= 148 + 100$$
$$= 248 \text{ bytes}$$
$$D(F \rightarrow F') = S(F) + L(F)$$
$$= 60 + 60$$
$$= 120 \text{ bytes}$$

Applying equation 1 to these distances, we obtain the PTIO probabilities shown in Figure 17–7.

Segment to Physical Parent.   Applying equation 3 to the example at hand, the following average distances from a segment back to its physical parent can be calculated:

$$D(B \rightarrow A) = D(A \rightarrow B) + \frac{(F(B) - 1) \times S(B)}{2}$$

$$= 240 + \frac{(2 - 1) \times 520}{2}$$

$$= 500 \text{ bytes}$$

Segment	PCIO	PTIO	PPIO
A	1.00	1.00	
B	.14	.32	
C	.14	.23	
D	.26	.14	
E	.71	.14	
F	.09	.07	

Figure 17–7. Estimated PCIO and PTIO probabilities.

$$D(C \rightarrow B) = D(B \rightarrow C) + \frac{(F(C) - 1 \times S(C)}{2}$$

$$= 240 + \frac{(1.5 - 1) \times 200}{2}$$

$$= 290 \text{ bytes}$$

$$D(D \rightarrow B) = D(B \rightarrow D) + \frac{(F(D) - 1) \times S(D)}{2}$$

$$= 460 + \frac{(1.5 - 1) \times 120}{2}$$

$$= 490 \text{ bytes}$$

$$D(E \rightarrow A) = D(A \rightarrow E) + \frac{(F(E) - 1 \times S(E)}{2}$$

$$= 1340 + \frac{(3 - 1) \times 148}{2}$$

$$= 1488 \text{ bytes}$$

$$D(F \rightarrow E) = D(E \rightarrow F) + \frac{(F(F) - 1 \times S(F)}{2}$$

$$= 160 + \frac{(.8 - 1) \times 60}{2}$$

$$= 154 \text{ bytes}$$

Applying equation 1 to these average distances, the PPIO probabilities shown in Figure 17–8 are obtained.

EXPECTED DL/I CALLS AND PHYSICAL I/OS

In a sense the I/O probabilities we have developed serve to evaluate one data-base design against another. But a full measure of the performance characteristics of a data base is not achieved until it is eval-

Segment	PCIO	PTIO	PPIO
A	1.00	1.00	—
B	.14	.32	.29
C	.14	.23	.17
D	.26	.14	.28
E	.71	.14	.86
F	.09	.07	.09

Figure 17–8. Estimated PCIO, PTIO, and PPIO probabilities.

uated in the context of the way it will be used. Thus we must now consider DL/I call patterns and times for the expected I/O operations.

Up to this point, we have worked with an average data-base record to simplify the analytic calculations. But evaluating data-base performance requires additional information about the physical design and the storage patterns of the data base as well as information about the usage to which it will be put. And much of this information can only be obtained by further assumptions or by simulation or modeling.

In order to present the concepts involved and to illustrate them with an example, several simplifying assumptions will be made in the material to follow. These assumptions are heavily dependent on the characteristics of the access method being used as well as on other physical design parameters; hence, the material to follow is more indicative than definitive. Bear in mind that with computer assistance, these assumptions can be avoided by simulating the rules of DL/I and its actions on the data base. The only inputs needed are the physical and logical DBDs (possibly with supplemental information of expected segment distributions) and the DL/I call patterns to be applied to the data bases.

Still, we are working with averages and probabilities, and the effects of contention are being ignored. Modeling on a computer is therefore recommended when more precise evaluations are required.

DL/I Call Patterns

Assume a sequence of DL/I calls as illustrated in Figure 17–9. For a given occurrence of segment A, we wish to update all occurrences of its E segments. We will do this for 100 different As, expecting to find 80 percent of the As that we seek. For the 20 percent that are not found, we will insert one A and one E segment.

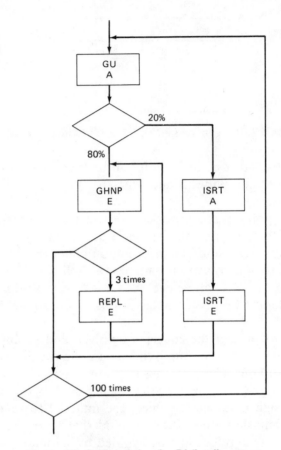

Figure 17–9. Example of a DL/I call pattern.

From the flowchart of Figure 17-9, we see that there will be 100 GET UNIQUEs (GU) to segment A. Expecting 20 percent of these calls to return a "not found" status, we expect to do 20 INSERTs (ISRT) of a new segment A and 20 ISRTs of a new segment E. Eighty entries are made to the loop for updating the E segments. Since on average there are three occurrences of segment E for each segment A, we expect to invoke the GET HOLD NEXT WITHIN PARENT (GHNP) and the REPLACE (REPL) 240 times each. We further expect 80 of the GHNPs to be PCIO (A to E) and 160 to be PTIO (E to E'). Actually, for each set of traversals of the update loop, there is a fourth GHNP, making an additional 80 GHNPs, that returns a "not found" status. This fourth GHNP does not cause an

I/O, so we will disregard it. The expected numbers of DL/I calls in this example are summarized in Figure 17–10.

Having determined the expected number of DL/I calls, we now calculate the expected number of physical I/Os and record these results in Figure 17–11.

Each GU to a root segment is classed as a Parent–to–Child I/O (PCIO = 1). Therefore, 100 I/Os will be expected for the root segment A.

From each A the first access to E will be a Parent–to–Child (PCIO = .71), and the other two expected accesses to E will be Segment–to–Twin (PTIO = .14). Thus the expected number of I/Os for the GHNPs to E is 80 × .71 + 160 × .14 = 79.20, which we will round up to 80.

Since each E that is located will be updated, every retrieved block containing an E will be updated. Hence the number of physical I/Os for REPLs will equal the expected number of I/Os for the GHNPs (i.e., 80).

To estimate the number of physical I/Os for the ISRTs, we need to know a little more about how the segments are stored by the access method being used. We are assuming the HDAM access method. Assume that none of the E segments are in the HDAM Root Addressable Area. Assume further that there are five root segments in an HDAM block, that there are 100 blocks in the Root Addressable Area, and that there are 200 blocks in the Overflow area. These parameters will all have been specified previously when constructing the DBD. Also assume that the blocks receiving inserts remain in the buffers until the end of processing (i.e., IMS sync point) when they are all written out.

Segment	GU	GHNP	REPL	ISRT
A	PC 100	——	——	20
B	——	——	——	——
C	——	——	——	——
D	——	——	——	——
E	——	PC 80	240	20
		PT 160	——	
		+80	——	
F	——	——	——	——

Figure 17–10. Expected number of DL/I calls.

Segment	GU	GHNP	REPL	ISRT
A	100	——	——	38
B	——	——	——	——
C	——	——	——	——
D	——	——	——	——
E	——	80	80	42
F	——			

Figure 17–11. Expected number of physical I/Os.

Now if a well-performing randomizing algorithm is used, it is equally likely that a root key will randomize to any block in the Root Addressable Area. Assume that there is space for it in the selected block. To calculate the expected number of blocks changed, we first calculate the probability that a given block is not changed, subtract that probability from one, and multiply the result by the number of blocks. This yields the following equation:

$$E \text{ (changed blocks)} = Nb \times \left(1 - \left(\frac{Nb - 1}{Nb} \right)^{Ni} \right) \quad (4)$$

where Ni is the number of root segments to be inserted, and Nb is the number of blocks in the Root Addressable Area. Applying equation 4 to the root segment inserts, we have:

$$E \text{ (changed blocks)} = 100 \times \left(1 - \left(\frac{99}{100} \right)^{20} \right)$$

$$= 18 \text{ blocks}$$

Thus in making 20 root segment inserts, we expect to update 18 blocks. We read the block, update it, and at the end of the process we write it back; therefore, we expect to make $18 \times 2 = 36$ physical I/Os. We do not use the I/O probabilities of Figure 17–8 because, after a physical address is computed by the randomizing routine, reference is made directly to the addressed block after first consulting the bit map. We also·may update the bit map, which is in main memory at this time. Allowing two more I/Os, one to read the bit map at the beginning of the process and one to write the bit map at the end of the process, we now estimate a total of 38 physical I/Os for inserting the 20 root segments. To be complete, we should also consider that inserts may cause additional I/Os for updating indexes. With HDAM there is no index, so we finalize the estimate of 38 physical I/Os.

Estimating the number of physical I/Os for dependent segments is even more elusive. DL/I would like to place the E segments into the same block as their root segments, but we have already assumed a byte limit that does not admit the E segments into the Root Addressable Area blocks. Therefore, on the basis of 20 inserts of E uniformly distributed over 200 overflow area blocks, equation 4 can be employed again to yield an expectation of 19 blocks changed. Doubling this number gives 38 I/Os to read and to write each of these blocks. But in addition to inserting the segment itself, pointers in parent segments and in surrounding twin segments must be updated when using the HD organizations, and the blocks containing some of these segments may not already be in the buffer pools. (Or if using HISAM, segments may have to be moved.) We will assume that, of the 20 inserts of segment E, 20 percent will require an additional I/O. Thus the total number of I/Os becomes 42. These estimates are summarized in Figure 17-11.

At best the accuracy of estimates such as those used above is quite uncertain. Physical I/O probabilities for insertions (and for deletions) are very difficult to estimate precisely. If they are critical to the evaluation, the modeling procedures discussed in the next chapter are recommended. But the estimates made thus far are usually adequate for gross evaluations, and the I/O probabilities for the three basic I/O operations are particularly helpful for studying the effect of searching long twin chains.

CPU AND PHYSICAL I/O TIMINGS

Having estimated the number of DL/I calls and the number of physical I/Os, we now turn our attention to the questions of CPU times and I/O times for the DL/I calls. Up to this point we have accompanied these performance concepts with a numerical example to illustrate the computations that can be performed and to show the assumptions (or simulation) that are required. But to avoid specifying speeds for specific hardware and software products, we will merely indicate the timing considerations.

For each type of DL/I call against a segment, CPU time is estimated multiplying the number of calls and the path length, and then dividing by the CPU speed. We have:

CPU time $= E(DL/I) \times PL / MIPS$
where:

E (DL/I) = expected number of DL/I calls (from Figure 17–10)

PL = path length (average number of instructions per call)

MIPS = CPU speed (instructions per microsecond)

I/O time is obtained by multiplying the number of physical I/Os by the sum of the expected seek time, the latency time, and the transfer time:

I/O time $= E(I/O) \times (ST + LT + XT)$
where:

E(I/O) = expected physical I/Os (from Figure 17–11)

ST = seek time (see below)

LT = latency time (time for 1/2 disk revolution)

XT = transfer time (block size divided by device speed)

Seek time is obtained by estimating the number of seeks and the length of each seek. The length is estimated in terms of cylinders traveled and then converted to travel time. These parameters depend on the storage patterns, the device characteristics, and the pattern of DL/I calls, from which the arm movement back and forth between segments can be derived. They can be roughly estimated analytically or by simulation for nonshared devices. For shared devices, where other activities are competing for the same access arm, seek time is best obtained by modeling, although it is often estimated as a single overall average value.

One of the most important aspects of performance evaluations is identifying and evaluating the portions of the data base involved in the most frequent number of accesses or in the searching of long twin chains or in both. It is by comparing the times or the probabilities for these areas against their counterparts from other designs or call pattern variations that we determine which design to accept, even though the rejected design may have been better in some of the less frequent activities. Computer assistance can provide the information, but at the current state of the art, it is still best for the human designer to make the judgments.

SUMMARY

For these analytic calculations, necessary simplifying assumptions have been made such as average data-base-record size and average distance traveled. Because of these assumptions, there is a rather wide confidence band about the calculated results. These calculations deal with CPU timings and physical I/O timings, but they give no information about contention aspects such as lockouts, channel and device busy, or increased seek times.

   The purpose of this chapter is to suggest a methodology and a technique. More precise results are available from more precise assumptions and derivations. However, experience indicates that the methods herein illustrated are effective in helping eliminate the more grossly inefficient designs. The remaining design variations can then be thoroughly evaluated under actual operating conditions by modeling.

18
APPLICATION PROGRAM MODELING

PHILOSOPHY

We have seen, in Chapter 17, some of the difficulties of estimating values and probabilities of the various parameters that must be considered in data-base performance evaluation. More precise evaluations can be obtained by modeling the data base and its application functions in a "live" environment.

Evaluation

To be more precisely evaluated, the design of a data base must be studied in the context of the use to which it will be put. In the sterile environment of analytic evaluation, we can determine on a gross level that one data-base design requires less space than another, or that one design should perform better than another. But exercising prototype models of the remaining candidate designs, and performing I/O calls via the actual data-base management system, is still the best means of determining the final design. Working with actual DL/I calls, with actual data-base records rather than with "average" records, and in an environment where normal contention for data-base resources is present, we can choose the most appropriate design with a high degree of confidence.

With regard to DL/I data bases, we propose creating and loading a prototype model of the data base, creating models of the application functions that will use the data base, executing these models in an IMS (or DOS-DL/I) system, performing actual DL/I calls against the data base, collecting statistics of times and counts and buffer pool activity at appropriate places, and evaluating the results. We are actually evaluating two different but related things: (1) the data-base design itself and (2) the application program's use of the data base.

Data-Base Design Evaluation.   Evaluation of the data base involves an evaluation of both the logical and physical design criteria. It can also be an evaluation of the data base's ability to grow. Examples of logical design evaluation can include such things as studying the effects of adding or deleting segment occurrences, adding or deleting segment types, modifying segment structure, and adding new reports and new functions. The left-to-right ordering of segments and other variations of the hierarchical structure can be studied.

Physical design evaluations can study variations in logical relations and secondary indexes and their effectiveness for various search strategies. Physical versus virtual pairing can be evaluated. Data set groups may be subjects of additional study. DBD parameters such as pointer options, block or logical record sizes, size of the Root Addressable Area, and the number of Root Anchor Points can similarly be evaluated.

Application Program Call Pattern Evaluation.   In many cases of poor data-base performance, the culprit has not been the data base itself but the use being made of it. As a simple example, if an application program begins an update sequence with a GHU followed by a REPL, and 80 percent of the time the desired segment is not there but must be inserted, the program is making inefficient use of the structure and existing content of the data base. Further, by collecting activity against certain segments, the call patterns may be able to take advantage of current buffer pool contents to reduce the actual number of physical I/Os. Variations of DL/I call patterns and buffer pool activity can be evaluated for given data-base designs.

Types of Modeling

Two types, or levels of sophistication, of modeling are recommended: (1) a preliminary modeling simply for path verification and (2) a detailed modeling for performance analysis.

Path Verification.   Even though path verification can be performed by analytic methods, confirmation can be obtained at very little added cost by actual DL/I calls. Each application program's ability to access its required segment types can be reported along with statistics about the number of successful and unsuccessful calls for each segment type, and diagnostics can be provided for call failures.

Detailed Timing Evaluation. Detailed timings of the DL/I calls constitute the heart of the modeling concept. Under actual operating conditions, we want to evaluate how much CPU time and elapsed time are required for each type of DL/I call, for groups of calls, and for the entire function. We also want to compare these times with those obtained from variations in the data-base design or size or in the application's use of the data base or in the buffer pool activity.

The Evaluation Procedure

This book takes the position that at this time performance evaluation is a subjective rather than an objective endeavor, and that it is best accomplished by human judgement rather than by automated calculation and comparison. There is no one parameter that best characterizes data-base performance. Also, to select a specific group of parameters, assign weights to them, and process them to obtain a single measure of performance, is itself a subjective exercise. At the present state of the art, the role of computer assistance is in the modeling. The evaluation still belongs to the human designer. But if the computer assistance has done its job well, the designer has the kind of information needed and in the formats needed.

Therefore we recommend the following approach to modeling and evaluation (Figure 18–1). The modeling and the reporting of the results are the automated parts of the process. The rest, especially observing and comparing the results, is a human endeavor.

MODELING INPUTS

Two types of input are required for modeling procedures. A description of the data base(s) to be modeled is required, along with a description of the application program's expected use of the data bases(s).

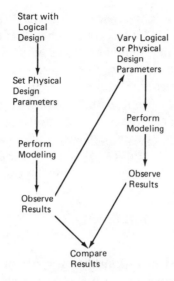

Figure 18-1. Manual comparison of modeling results.

Data Base

As with the analytic space and time estimates, the data base to be modeled can be described by DBD statements with appropriate supplemental information. Primarily, this added information will consist of segment distributions and key value distributions. We have already discussed the reasons for providing segment distributions. The key value distributions are used to control the probability of finding the desired segment in each data-base call. This also means they can be used to guarantee a "hit" when necessary, such as when accessing a destination parent. From this type of input, the modeling procedures can automatically allocate and load the model data bases.

Application Program

A working model of the application programs must also be provided. What is needed are programs in load-module form that invoke actual DL/I calls against the prototype data base, simulate the logic of the application, and perform measurements from which I/O timings and other performance statistics can be derived. Macro extensions to the common programming languages (such as COBOL, PL/I, and Assembler) can be provided to simplify the task of preparing such models. Special modeling languages have also been devised for this purpose. One advantage of using the macro extensions is that when the modeling is completed, a running program is in existence in a language familiar to the application programmers. By removing the timing and measurement macros and inserting detailed program logic, a production application can very easily be obtained. In addition to the application model, of course, a PSB to describe the model's data-base requirements must also be provided.

APPLICATION PROGRAM MODELING CONSIDERATIONS

To provide the desired measurements for performance evaluation, the application program models must contain certain features. The features (or capabilities) of primary interest are suggested in the next section and then illustrated by an example.

Basic Modeling Features

The objective in application program modeling is to prepare a prototype model that simulates as closely as possible the program's logic and call pattern structure and that collects useful performance information. Six basic modeling features are vital to such a prototype:

1. Actual DL/I calls. The major ingredients of the prototype model are the DL/I call patterns to be executed. The primary purpose is to evaluate the efficiency of these call patterns on the data base that has been designed and to determine areas for tuning or redesign.
2. Time delays. Time delays are used to approximate the time required for internal application processing between DL/I calls.
3. Branching. Branching is used to simulate the decision making and looping of the application. Various types of branching can be used. I/O branching can be based on DL/I status codes. Statistical branching (e.g., 80% to A, 20% to B) can simulate

random processes. Value branching can be done based on the values of parameters, counts, or other statistics.

4. Program statistics collection. Various statistics can be collected. Elapsed and CPU times of individual DL/I calls, of groups of calls, and of entire processes can be collected. Counts of the number of traversals of selected paths can be gathered. Values of interesting parameters from status registers or from calculations can be recorded at specified time intervals or for specified path traversals. Besides being reported, these statistics can be accumulated and compared, and branching within the application model can be done accordingly. They can also be used as parameters in subsequent calculations. The capability should be present for these statistics to be accumulated for the duration of the run or to be reset at specified times.

5. Buffer pool statistics collection. The contents of the VSAM and the ISAM/OSAM buffer pools should also be collected at appropriate intervals in order to study the actual physical I/Os resulting from the DL/I calls.

6. Statistics reporting. Macros should be available to report selected statistics at any point in the model. They can be reported graphically or tabularly, and in detail or as means, deviations, maximums, and so forth. The option of resetting or continuing to accumulate should be part of this feature.

Modeling Example

Figure 18–2 gives a simple example of the use of most of these basic features in application program modeling. This is an example of an update operation in which the application program expects the required segment to be present most of the time. It starts with a GU and expects to follow with a REPL. Should the GU fail, it inserts a new segment. The entire update process is repeated 100 times. To approximate internal processing times, time-delay macros are included before the ISRT (10 microseconds) and after each update iteration (50 microseconds). Arrows indicate places to insert additional macros to record the times of each DL/I call, time for the overall process, and counts of actual traversals of the REPL and the ISRT paths. Finally, after 100 iterations, selected statistics are printed.

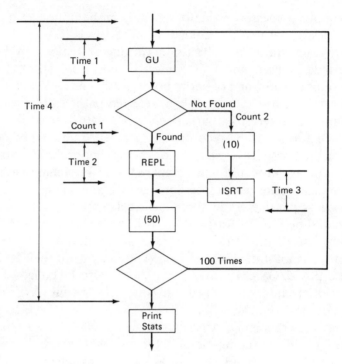

Figure 18-2. Example of DL/I call pattern.

DATA-BASE MODELING

The following are the primary considerations required for successful modeling of the data base itself.

Generation and Loading

From the physical and logical DBDs (and their supplemental information), the modeling programs can derive all the needed data-base characteristics, and the data bases can be generated, allocated, and loaded automatically. The necessary Job Control Language can be automatically generated to perform these functions, calling on IMS utility programs as needed.

Segment Content

The segments loaded into these newly created data bases need contain only key field values. (Here we are using "key" loosely to mean all search fields regardless of whether or not they are defined as sequence fields.) Values for non-key fields need not be included. The purpose of the application model is to evaluate data-base performance; therefore it need not be interested in segment content after segments have been located and retrieved.

Segment Key Values

The designer must specify (directly or indirectly) the values of the key fields for the occurrences of each segment type to be accessed. The ability should be present for the designer to supply exact key values or to specify statistical or empirical distributions from which the key values can be generated automatically. For example, the designer may want the key field of one set of segment occurrences to contain values generated randomly in increments of 10 and uniformly distributed between 0 and 80. In response to this specification, the modeling programs might use a random number generator to generate key values of 10, 20, 10, 40, 50, 20, 60, 60, 50, 40, 0, 70, 40, 30, 60, 80, and so on, depending on the number of segment occurrences.

While generating these key values, the generating routines can build tables of the generated key values for use in controlling the hit ratios of the DL/I calls to be made against the various segments.

Random and Guaranteed Hits

The capability must exist for specifying random (or statistical) hits for certain segment types. For example, the designer may want to specify that the occurrences of a certain segment type are to be found 80 percent of the time and not found 20 percent of the time. Assuming the segment key values are distributed from 0 to 80 in increments of 10 (as demonstrated in the preceding section), this hit ratio can be accomplished by generating random key values for the Segment

Search Argument (SSA) that range from 0 to 100 in increments of
10. Many other types of hit ratios can also be obtained according to
desired statistical patterns of other criteria.

On the other hand, tables of the existing key values can be used
to assure guaranteed hits. By randomly or sequentially selecting a
key value from the appropriate table and inserting it into the SSA
as a search argument, random or sequential accesses can be made
with the hit guaranteed. There are at least four places where guaranteed hits are required: (1) locating logical parents, (2) locating
physical parents, (3) locating targets of secondary indexes, and (4)
locating segment occurrences that are otherwise known to exist. For
these purposes, tables of concatenated key values can be built by the
key generating routines.

Finally, making additional accesses to segment occurrences previously accessed can be accomplished by having the application
model save the concatenated keys of these segments for future use.

Physical Pairing.   If physically paired segments are to be present in
the data bases, special care is required in generating their key values
to assure that a search key that produces a hit in one will also produce a hit in the other and vice versa. Note that their concatenated
keys will *not* be the same. Reference 8 describes one technique for
obtaining key compatibility between the paired segment occurrences.

OUTPUTS

Many types of information can be reported by the application model
to show the performance characteristics of the data base as it is being
used. The following sections give a representative sampling of available information that can be useful for performance evaluation. It
can be presented in tabular form as detailed lists or as means, distributions, maxima, or minima. Graphic presentations and histo-
grams are especially recommended.

I/O and Program Timings

CPU and elapsed times can be reported by segment type and call
type for specified calls and segments. They can also be reported for

groups of call sequences, for portions of the application model, and for the entire processing of a function.

DL/I status code summaries can also be presented showing the patterns of successful and unsuccessful calls for the various segment types.

DL/I Call Analyses

DL/I calls to selected segments can be selectively traced by printing the contents of the Program Communication Block (PCB), Input-Output Area (IOA), and the SSA. Both the status code and the key feedback area from the PCB are especially useful in analyzing the call activity.

Counts and Values

Counts and ratios of traversals of selected paths in the model, as well as counts and statistics of the number of executions of selected program instructions, can be reported. Values of registers and results of calculations within the application model can provide information about situations of special interest to the designer. Current values within the run and final values at the end of the run should be available.

Buffer Pool Statistics

VSAM and ISAM/OSAM buffer pool statistics provide especially helpful information for performance evaluation. The number and sizes of buffer pools are critical in determining how frequently blocks are read into and written from the pools. The number of DL/I calls satisfied from within the buffer pools is of utmost importance. The number of space and background writes to free buffers for additional reads is also very important. These statistics can be printed at the end of the run, at checkpoint times, or at other specified intervals.

REFERENCES

The following references provide additional and more detailed insights into many of the topics presented in this book. These references are recommended to those who want to obtain more detailed knowledge and understanding of DL/I data bases.

1. Date, C. J. *An Introduction to Data Base Systems*. 3d ed. Reading, Mass.: Addison-Wesley, 1981.
2. Dechow, E., and D. Lundberg. *The IMS Data Base Application Design Review*. IBM report G320-6009 (1977).
3. GUIDE International Corporation. *The Data Base Design Guide*. 1974.
4. Hoyt, S. *IMS/VS/MVS Performance and Tuning Guide*. IBM technical bulletin G320-6004 (1980).
5. Hubbard, G. U. *Computer-Assisted Data Base Design*. New York: Van Nostrand, 1981.
6. IBM Corporation. *IMS/VS Version 1 Application Programming: Designing and Coding*. Publication no. SH20-9026 (1981).
7. ———. *IMS/VS Version 1 Data Base Administration Guide*. Publication no. SH20-9025 (1981).
8. IBM Corporation, DBPROTOTYPE/II Program Description/Operations Manual, Publication no. SH20-1953 (1983).
9. Kroneke, D. *Data Base Processing*. Science Research Associates, 1983.
10. Lewis, R. Z. *Performance Considerations for IMS/VS 1.2 Data Sharing*. IBM technical bulletin GS20-5943 (1983).
11. McElreath, T. J. *IMS Design and Implementation Techniques*. Q.E.D. Information Sciences, 1979.
12. Schramm, D. A. *Managing IMS Performance via IMS Control Block and Buffer Pool Statistics*. IBM technical bulletin GG22-9013 (1978).
13. Teorey, T. J., and J. P. Fry. *Design of Data Base Structures*. Englewood Cliffs, N.J.: Prentice-Hall, 1982.
14. Wiederhold, G. *Database Design*. New York: McGraw-Hill, 1977.

INDEX